A MESSIANIC HAGGADA

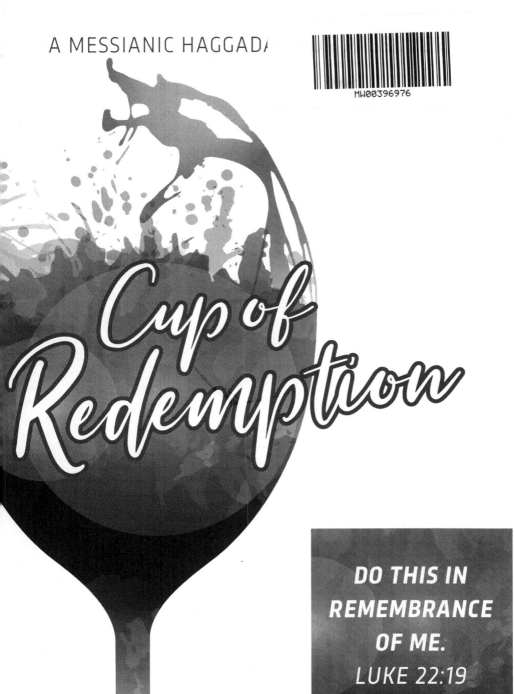

Cup of Redemption

DO THIS IN
REMEMBRANCE
OF ME.
LUKE 22:19

HOPE. DELIVERANCE. REVELATION

Emet HaTorah
PO Box 28281, Macon, GA 31221-8281 USA
www.emethatorah.com

Comments and questions: www.emethatorah.com/contact

DARREN N. HUCKEY

Cup of Redemption

Emet
HaTorah

Connecting disciples of Yeshua with the eternal Torah of God

Invitation

CELEBRATING REDEMPTION

Tonight we celebrate redemption. Tonight we celebrate the redemption of the Children of Israel through the exodus event as they have been doing for over three thousand years. However, Passover is not an exclusively Jewish experience. Non-Jewish disciples of Yeshua also find great meaning in the Passover seder. Just as the Israelites were freed from the slavery of the Egyptians, followers of Yeshua have been released from the bondage of sin. The Apostle Paul says that the Gentiles who have come to faith are predestined "for adoption to himself as sons through Jesus Christ," and that they find "redemption through his blood, the forgiveness of our trespasses, according to the riches of his grace" (Ephesians 1:5, 7). And although Gentiles disciples of Yeshua are not considered Jewish, Paul says that they do have an elevated status that brings them into the family of Israel in some capacity:

> Therefore remember that at one time you Gentiles in the flesh, called "the uncircumcision" by what is called the circumcision, which is made in the flesh by hands—remember that you were at that time separated from Christ, alienated from the commonwealth of Israel and strangers to the covenants of promise, having no hope and without God in the world. But now in Christ Jesus you who once were far off have been brought near by the blood of Christ. (Ephesians 2:11–13)

Gentile disciples of Yeshua are engrafted into the root of the Jewish people (Romans 11). They have left their past and taken on a new identity as they have come under the kingship of the Jewish Messiah. They have joined themselves to the physical descendants of Abraham, Isaac, and Jacob. Therefore, we can also use this opportunity to celebrate the deliverance of the Gentile disciples of Yeshua from the dominion of darkness to the Kingdom of Light. Tonight we celebrate redemption.

TASTING REDEMPTION

Tonight we also "eat redemption." We can learn about the exodus from the Scriptures, books, films, lectures and sermons. However, we learn in quite a different way when personally experiencing Passover. Tonight we experience redemption first hand. Tonight we "eat redemption."

Tonight we suffer as slaves in the land of Egypt. Tonight we are delivered from the hand of Pharaoh. Tonight we celebrate the victory of God as He parts the waters of the Sea of Reeds to allow us to cross over. Tonight, much different from all other nights, we become more aware of who we are as a chosen people, a royal priesthood, called out from among the peoples of the earth. For on a night such as this, we went forth out of Egypt, leaving behind our lives as nameless slaves. On a night such as this we rejoiced in our newly found freedom and identity. On a night such as this Messiah Yeshua experienced our pain and passion in the final hours before His crucifixion, which would ultimately lead to our redemption. Tonight we share the sorrow as well as the joy of our ancestors, the natural branches of Israel, as we remember what we should never forget …

WE ONCE WERE SLAVES...
BUT NOW WE ARE FREE!!!

And when the hour came, he reclined at table, and the apostles with him. And he said to them, "I have earnestly desired to eat this Passover with you before I suffer."

(Luke 22:14-15)

Cup of Redemption Haggadah

About Passover

WELCOME

Welcome to Passover! You've just embarked on a journey that will become a memory for the rest of your life. Tonight is a special occasion that will take you back nearly 3,500 years in history to relive an experience of deliverance and freedom. Join us tonight in celebration of this momentous event that we call the Passover Seder.

WHAT IS A SEDER?

Seder is a Hebrew word that means "set order." It is the specific order of ceremony for a given event, and it has a special association with the ritual revolving around the Passover meal. The Passover Seder is designed to recall, memorialize, and relive the events of the exodus of the Children of Israel from their slavery in Egypt. The main elements of the seder are: Unleavened bread, bitter herbs, wine, lamb and the Maggid (the telling of the exodus event). Each of these elements are an important component in the seder. Our seder, however, will also include references to the last days of Yeshua's earthly ministry in order to connect us with his final seder meal that he shared with his disciples. It will also remind us how Yeshua symbolizes the Passover lamb. We will accomplish all of this by means of the haggadah.

THE HAGGADAH

The haggadah is the book that you are now reading. This is what will guide us through the ceremony of the seder. The word "haggadah" is a Hebrew word that means "telling." The haggadah will tell us everything that we need to know for our event, as well as tell us the story of the exodus. This book is by no means a rigid structure of how you should conduct every moment of your seder. It should, however, provide a basic framework for you to create your own unique experience. Feel free to personalize this experience by minimizing some sections and emphasizing other sections that are more meaningful to you. Make it personal, make it fun, and make it memorable. More on this aspect in the Dor L'dor section.

IN REMEMBRANCE OF ME

Participating in a Passover seder meal is a reminder of who we are as a redeemed people. It is first a fulfillment of an instruction in the Torah for those whose ancestors were literally redeemed from Egypt. However, it is also a means by which disciples of Yeshua "proclaim the Lord's death until he comes" (1 Corinthians 11:26). Yeshua told his disciples, "I have earnestly desired to eat this Passover with you before I suffer" (Luke 22:15). By celebrating the Passover with a seder meal we are connecting to our Messiah, identifying with him in his suffering, and rejoicing over his resurrection. May the LORD bless you and your home as you embark on this wonderful journey.

TIMING

When should we celebrate Passover and the Feast of Unleavened Bread? The easiest way is to find Passover on a Jewish calendar. In the biblical reckoning of time, a day begins at sunset. Therefore, the Seder begins at sunset, at the onset of the 15th of Nisan. This also begins the Festival of Unleavened Bread, or Chag HaMatzot. The Festival of Unleavened Bread is seven days long, and the first and the seventh of the festival are designated as special Sabbaths (Leviticus 23:7–8). We set apart, or sanctify, these days by refraining from many of our normal activities.

COME ONE, COME ALL

It is traditional to celebrate Passover with family and friends. It is therefore very appropriate to invite guests to celebrate Passover with you. Passover is a commemoration of the work of salvation, and salvation should always be a shared experience. This goes back to the biblical times where the Passover lamb was required to be shared by several people so that it would not be wasted. The haggadah proclaims, "Whoever is hungry, let him come and eat; whoever is in need, let him come and join in celebrating Passover." There will always be those who are hungry, both physically and spiritually, and it is our responsibility as disciples of our Master to feed them. We open our homes to those who would desire to eat from our tables both physical and spiritual food.

LEAVEN

Leaven is the quintessential representation of sin, and therefore must be purged from our homes prior to the evening of the seder meal. It should be removed the day prior to the seder. It must not only be removed, it must not be in our possession, as it says, "No leavened bread shall be seen with you, and no leaven shall be seen with you in all your territory" (Exodus 13:7). Setting it in the garage won't do. It must be thrown away or destroyed. If you would like to cleanse your home according to the ritual custom, it has been included in the haggadah. Also, since Scripture specifically says that during this seven-day period that we should eat matzah, we should eat at least some matzah each day of the feast.

WHERE'S THE MEAT?

In the days of the Bible, the *Pesach* (the Paschal/Passover lamb) was the focal point of the Passover seder. However, since there is no Temple today, lamb is no longer eaten at the seder meal. Since it is forbidden to make a sacrifice without the Temple (see Deuteronomy 16:5–7), eating lamb at a ritual meal such as this would be in violation of a fundamental precept of the Torah. The shank bone is symbolic of the missing Passover lamb, and the roasted egg is symbolic of the festival meat that would be a large portion of the meal (for more information on this, see "Beitzah" on page 85). Therefore, we forego eating lamb at the seder and use the afikoman as the focal point today, allowing its taste to linger in our mouths at the end of the seder meal.

AFI-WHAT?

The afikoman (pronounced "ah-fee-KOH-man") is the focal point of the Passover seder. The word afikoman is a Hebrew word that was transliterated from Greek and means, "that which comes after" or simply "dessert." The afikoman is the substitute for the Passover sacrifice, which was the last thing eaten at the seder during the of the Holy Temple. Since the afikoman represents the Passover lamb, the Talmud states that it is forbidden to have any other food after the afikoman, so that the taste of the afikoman remains in our mouths.

A FOREIGN AFFAIR

The Passover Seder can seem like an extremely foreign affair as we attempt to engage in this ancient Middle Eastern festivity. Although we are supposed to relate the events of the Passover in terms that our modern, Western minds can understand, we should also be filled with a sense of wonderment as we participate in this ancient ritual. It is supposed to take us back and help us reconnect with the rich soil from which the roots of our faith have sprung. If it feels strange and foreign, it is because it is supposed to be. Be sure to appreciate this strangeness, rather than be hindered by it.

DOR L'DOR

The Hebrew expression "dor l'dor" means "from generation to generation." This is how the Passover is supposed to be remembered and celebrated. It is a time to transfer an experience from one generation to the next. Many of the traditions that revolve around the seder meal have been added for the sake of arousing the curiosity of the children and keeping their attention. This night should be focused on transmitting the story and meaning of the exodus to our children in a fun, engaging manner. If the text of the haggadah is above the heads of your children or if the long sections of reading will lose their attention, revise it to capture their imaginations through the use of illustrations, games and other playful innovations. Bottom line—make it fun and memorable!

FAST OF THE FIRSTBORN

As an act of gratitude for sparing their lives, it is tradition for the firstborn males of each family to fast the day prior to Passover. In households where the firstborn boys are under the age of thirteen, their fathers fast on their behalf.

FOUR CUPS

Through the course of the seder meal, four cups of wine (or grape juice) are consumed. Ideally, each of the four cups should be fully consumed. However, if you are not able to do so, then the first cup should be drank completely and at least half of the subsequent cups drank. The four cups are symbolic and correspond to four promises that God made with the Children of Israel in Exodus 6:6-7 before He delivered them from Egypt. These are known as the Four Expressions of Redemption. They are as follows:

Sanctification
"I will bring you out from under the burdens of the Egyptians" (Exodus 6:6)

Judgment
"I will deliver you from slavery" (Exodus 6:6)

Redemption
"I will redeem you with an outstretched arm and with great acts of judgment" (Exodus 6:6)

Kingship
"I will take you to be my people, and I will be your God" (Exodus 6:7)

The Seder Plate

There are many traditions as to how the seder plate is arranged and what elements appear on it. Here is an explanation of the various elements of the seder plate and some traditions associated with them.

Elements

OF THE SEDER PLATE

BEITZAH

Beitzah means "egg," and it is usually served boiled and "roasted." See "Beitzah" (page 85) for more information. The beitzah corresponds to the chagigah ("festival") offering of Passover.

Z'ROA

Z'roa means "arm," and is most often a roasted shankbone of a lamb. However, there are some customs that use a roasted chicken neck. It symbolizes the central Passover offering.

KARPAS

Karpas means "green vegetable." It can include: parsley, celery, lettuce, radishes, a boiled potato, a raw onion, or a variety of other options. The karpas serves as the appetizer and represents the newness of springtime.

MAROR

Maror means "bitter." Most often this is either freshly ground horseradish or Romaine lettuce. It symbolizes the bitterness of slavery. It is used to fulfill the obligation to eat "bitter herbs" (Exodus 12:8).

CHAZERET

Chazeret means "lettuce." This is another instance of maror and is most often Romaine lettuce. However, some customs use freshly ground horseradish. It is associated with the Hillel Sandwich and is used to fulfill the obligation to eat "matzah and bitter herbs" together (Exodus 12:8).*

CHAROSET

Charoset comes from the word cheres, which means "clay." This yummy mixture of fruit and nuts symbolizes the mortar the Hebrews used when they were enslaved in Egypt. We dip our matzah and maror into it, but shake the bulk of it off before eating. It is also added to the Hillel Sandwich.

---

*Although this phrase is a biblical commandment, we are unable to actually fulfill it today as specified in the Torah. The Torah states, "They shall eat the flesh that night, roasted on the fire; with unleavened bread and bitter herbs they shall eat it" (Exodus 12:8). The commandment is to eat the matzah and bitter herbs along with the Passover offering. Since we are no longer able to bring the Passover offering, this commandment cannot be fulfilled in actuality and has therefore been reduced to a means by which we remember this commandment.

Preparation

BEDIKAT CHAMETZ
THE SEARCH FOR LEAVEN

*A*ccording to Exodus 12:15; 13:7-8 no leaven is to be found in the house on the feast of Passover. Therefore great care is taken to insure all leaven is removed from the dwellings:

> Seven days you shall eat unleavened bread. On the first day you shall remove leaven out of your houses, for if anyone eats what is leavened, from the first day until the seventh day, that person shall be cut off from Israel. (Exodus 12:15)

> Unleavened bread shall be eaten for seven days; no leavened bread shall be seen with you, and no leaven shall be seen with you in all your territory. You shall tell your son on that day, 'It is because of what the LORD did for me when I came out of Egypt.' (Exodus 13:7-8)

Biblically, leaven often represents sin and observant Jews take special care to ensure that anything containing leaven be completely removed in order that it would not contaminate the home. Beginning one month prior to the feast of Passover, the Jewish woman goes through a very intensive house cleaning process to extract all the leaven from her home. All carpets and rugs are cleaned, the drapes and curtains, the entire house is vacuumed including between the seats of the couch and chairs, and between the box springs and mattress in the home. The cookware, flatware, and dishes that are used for the rest of the year are removed and a special set of cookware, flatware, and dishes are brought out. The set that is brought out is the very best that the family owns, since we are to give God our very best. All leaven has been removed from the home with the exception of ten pieces which are hidden throughout the house. On the evening before Passover, when all the lights in the house have been turned off, the father takes a feather, a wooden spoon, a candle, and a bag and performs the following ceremony.

As the ceremony begins the following blessing is recited:

Blessed are You, O LORD our God, King of the Universe, Who has sanctified us with His commandments and commanded us concerning the removal of chametz.

After saying the blessing and lighting the candle the father begins to search the home using the candle to search every crack and crevice of the house for the pieces of leaven. Once a piece of leaven is located, the father uses the feather to brush the leaven onto the wooden spoon. He then places the leaven into the bag. Once all pieces of leaven have been located and gathered into the bag, the bag is kept in a safe place until morning.

After the inspection has ended the following declaration is recited:

All chametz or leaven still in my possession, that I have not seen or have not removed because I have no knowledge of it, let it be ownerless like the dust of the earth.

BIUR CHAMETZ
BURNING OF THE LEAVEN

*T*he following morning (by mid-morning) the bag containing the leaven and articles used for its retrieval are gathered together and taken to where a fire has been prepared. It is then thrown into the flames where it is consumed—never again to be remembered or retrieved. While the chametz is burning the following confession is made:

Any chametz in my possession that I have seen or not, have noticed or not, have removed or not, shall be as if it does not exist, and ownerless as the dust of the earth.

Many times in Scripture leaven is symbolic of sin, especially pride. Just like pride, leaven puffs up anything that it comes in contact with. Our Heavenly Father examines every crack and crevice of our heart using His Word, symbolized by the candle. The light of the Word dispels darkness and reveals anything that is displeasing in His sight. His Holy Spirit, symbolized by the feather, then reveals to us our sin. Once we have this revelation, it is our job to repent. Some people see the wooden spoon as a symbol for the cross of Yeshua. When we repent, our Heavenly Father takes our sins and casts them away forever. This is symbolized by the burning of the bag. We can see how this custom is a vivid reminder of what the Apostle Paul had in mind when he wrote:

> Your boasting is not good. Do you not know that a little leaven leavens the whole lump? Cleanse out the old leaven that you may be a new lump, as you really are unleavened. For Christ, our Passover lamb, has been sacrificed. Let us therefore celebrate the festival, not with the old leaven, the leaven of malice and evil, but with the unleavened bread of sincerity and truth. (1 Corinthians 5:6-8)

It is not enough for the leaven to be out of the house, it must be out of the Jewish person's possession. This is even more important in regard to purging the leaven of sin from our lives.

The sixth chapter of Romans is Paul's discourse on freeing oneself from the clutches of sin ("leaven"). He uses the analogies of death and resurrection, slaves and freedmen. Following this, in the seventh chapter he goes back and forth with trying to explain the nature of struggling with sin. He culminates his argument in chapter eight, telling us that we must "put to death the misdeeds of the body" in order to be fully sons of God (vs. 12-14).

But on a practical level, how do we do this? We must do just as our Master has instructed us and regard even the smallest sin as leaven with the potential to spread throughout our entire being. We must purge the leaven of sin within us before it consumes us.[2]

---

1   Matthew 5-7

Lighting the Candles

"These are the appointed feasts of the Lord, the holy convocations, which you shall proclaim at the time appointed for them." (Leviticus 23:4)

The sanctity of Passover officially begins once the candles are lit. Candle lighting should be done at least 18 minutes prior to sunset, unless it is a Saturday night, in which case it should be done an hour after sundown.

THE WOMAN LIGHTS THE CANDLES AND RECITES THE FOLLOWING BLESSING. IF IT IS A FRIDAY NIGHT, THE WORDS IN PARENTHESES ARE ADDED.

בָּרוּךְ אַתָּה ה'
אֱלֹהֵינוּ מֶלֶךְ הָעוֹלָם
אֲשֶׁר קִדְּשָׁנוּ
בְּמִצְוֹתָיו וְצִוָּנוּ
לְהַדְלִיק נֵר שֶׁל
(שַׁבָּת וְ) יוֹם טוֹב.

Baruch ata Adonai

Eloheinu Melech

HaOlam asher kidshanu

b'mitzvotav v'tzivanu

l'hadlik neir shel

(Shabbat v') yom tov.

Blessed are You, O LORD our God, King of the Universe, Who has sanctified us by His commandments, and commanded us to light the (Sabbath and) festival lights.

Non-Jewish disciples of Yeshua should consider substituting the following blessing:

Blessed are You, O LORD our God, King of the Universe Who has created the (Sabbath and) festival lights.

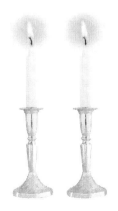

Order of Service

The Passover Seder consists of 15 steps which is said to represent the fifteen psalms in the "Song of Ascents" (Psalm 120-134), the psalms chanted by the Levites as they walked up the fifteen steps to the Temple.

1 Kaddesh
We say a blessing (kiddush) at the beginning of the seder over the first cup of wine in order to sanctify the day.

2 Urchatz
We ritually wash our hands before partaking of karpas.

3 Karpas
We dip the karpas into the salt water or red wine vinegar and eat it.

4 Yachatz
We break the matzah and separate the Afikoman.

5 Maggid
We tell the story of Pesach.

6 Rachtzah
We ritually wash our hands before eating bread (matzah).

7 Motzi
We bless God for the bread (matzah).

8 Matzah
We bless God for the commandment to eat matzah.

9 Maror
We bless God for the commandment to eat the bitter herbs.

10 Korech
We eat matzah and bitter herbs together (in the form of the "Hillel sandwich").

11 Shulchan Orech
We eat the festival meal together.

12 Tzafun
We find and eat the Afikoman.

13 Barech
We bless God for our food by reciting Grace After Meals.

14 Hallel
We recite Psalms of praise (Psalm 113-118) for this special occasion.

15 Nirtzah
We ask God to accept our prayers.

Kaddesh
SANCTIFICATION OF THE DAY

"On the fifteenth day of the same month is the Feast of Unleavened Bread to the LORD ... On the first day you shall have a holy convocation; you shall not do any ordinary work." (Leviticus 23:6–7)

THE FIRST CUP IS POURED.

Cup of Sanctification

"I will bring you out from under the burdens of the Egyptians." (Exodus 6:6)

The Cup of Sanctification "sanctifies" or sets apart this time as something dedicated to the LORD. It is done at the beginning of any special time consecrated to the Almighty. Tonight we set apart this time to remember how God set us apart from Egypt. Each participant's cup should be filled by someone else in order to invoke an elevated sense of awareness that we are no longer slaves. However, we serve one another, elevating each other in the process.

Blessings from the Didache (the early teachings of the Apostles to the Gentiles) are used in addition to the traditional blessings throughout the haggadah for both food and drink.

ON FRIDAY NIGHT BEGIN HERE. OTHERWISE, SKIP TO BLESSING FOR WINE. LEADER LIFTS CUP WITH RIGHT HAND.

LEADER: (Softly say: And there was evening and there was morning) The sixth day. Thus the heavens and the earth were finished, and all the host of them. And on the seventh day God finished his work that he had done, and he rested on the seventh day from all his work that he had done. So God blessed the seventh day and made it holy, because on it God rested from all his work that he had done in creation. (Genesis 1:31-2:3).

We thank You, our Father, for the holy vine of Your servant
David, that You made known to us through Your servant
Yeshua. To You be the glory forever. (Didache 9:2)

בָּרוּךְ אַתָּה ה'	*Baruch ata Adonai*	Blessed are You, O
אֱלֹהֵינוּ מֶלֶךְ	*Eloheinu Melech*	LORD our God, King of the Universe,
הָעוֹלָם בּוֹרֵא	*HaOlam borei*	Who creates the
פְּרִי הַגָּפֶן.	*p'ri hagafen.*	fruit of the vine.

LEAN TO THE LEFT WHILE DRINKING THE CUP OF WINE.

IF IT IS FRIDAY NIGHT INCLUDE THE WORDS IN BRACKETS.

LEADER: Blessed are You, O LORD our God, King of the Universe, Who has chosen us from every people, exalted us above every tongue, and sanctified us with His commandments. And You gave us, O LORD, our God, with love [Sabbaths for rest], appointed festivals for gladness, festivals and times for joy, [this Sabbath day and] this day of the Festival of Matzot, the time of our freedom [with love] for a holy convocation, a memorial of the exodus from Egypt. For You have chosen us and You have sanctified us above all the peoples, and You have given us as a heritage Your holy [Sabbath and] Festivals [in love and in favor] in gladness and in joy. Blessed are You, O LORD, Who sanctifies [the Sabbath and] Israel and the festive seasons.

IF IT IS SATURDAY NIGHT INCLUDE THIS BLESSING.

LEADER: Blessed are You, O LORD our God, King of the Universe Who created the lights of fire. Blessed are You, O LORD our God, King of the Universe, Who makes a distinction between the holy and profane, light and darkness, Israel and the nations, the Sabbath and the six workdays. You have made a distinction between the holiness of the Sabbath and the holiness of the festival, and You have sanctified the Sabbath above the six work-days. You have set apart and made holy Your people Israel with Your holiness. Blessed are You, O LORD, Who distinguishes between degrees of sanctity.

CONTINUE HERE ON ALL NIGHTS.

בָּרוּךְ אַתָּה ה'
אֱלֹהֵינוּ מֶלֶךְ הָעוֹלָם
שֶׁהֶחֱיָנוּ וְקִיְּמָנוּ
וְהִגִּיעָנוּ לַזְּמַן הַזֶּה.

*Baruch ata Adonai
Eloheinu Melech
HaOlam shehecheyanu
v'kiymanu v'higi'anu
laz'man ha-zeh.*

Blessed are You, O LORD our God, King of the Universe, Who has kept us alive, sustained us and enabled us to celebrate this season.

THE SECOND CUP OF WINE IS NOW POURED.

Urchatz
WASHING THE HANDS

"When they come near the altar to minister ... they shall wash with water." (Exodus 30:20)

For concerns about ritual hand washing, see "Ritual "Ritual Hand Washing" on page 89. Water is poured over each hand three times, beginning with the right hand.

WASH HANDS AT THIS TIME WITHOUT RECITING A BLESSING.

Karpas
DIPPING & EATING THE GREEN VEGETABLE

*"The people of Israel groaned because of their slavery and cried out for help.
Their cry for rescue from slavery came up to God." (Exodus 2:23)*

LEADER: The LORD's calendar is meant to teach us in our every day lives as we experience the changing of the seasons, and the festivals that He has established for each. He could have chosen winter, summer or fall in which to bring our Redemption, but the Holy One, Blessed be He, chose the springtime to remind us of our newly found freedom. The karpas is a symbol of springtime and of hope.

PARTICIPANT: Sometimes we despair of the wickedness in our world. Passover calls us to hope again.

LEADER: We dip the karpas once to remember the tears we cried in Egypt when we were slaves. May we never be so comfortable that we become complacent, forgetting the pain of others.

PARTICIPANT: "You shall not oppress a sojourner. You know the heart of a sojourner, for you were sojourners in the land of Egypt." [2]

---

2   Exodus 23:9

LEADER: We dip our karpas a second time to remember the drowning of the Egyptians in the Sea and the miraculous delivery of Israel.

בָּרוּךְ אַתָּה ה'
אֱלֹהֵינוּ מֶלֶךְ הָעוֹלָם
בּוֹרֵא פְּרִי הָאֲדָמָה.

Baruch ata Adonai

Eloheinu Melech HaOlam

borei p'ri ha-adama.

Blessed are You, O LORD our God, King of the Universe, Who creates the fruit of the earth.

DIP KARPAS TWICE INTO THE LIQUID (EITHER RED WINE VINEGAR OR SALT WATER) AND EAT ALL OF THE KARPAS WHILE LEANING TO THE LEFT.

Yachatz
BREAKING THE MATZAH

"When he had given thanks, he broke it, and said, 'This is my body, which is for you. Do this in remembrance of me.' " (1 Corinthians 11:24)

THE LEADER BREAKS THE MIDDLE MATZAH & WRAPS THE LARGER PIECE IN A NAPKIN OR PLACES IT IN AN AFIKOMAN BAG.

LEADER: Of the three Matzot on the Seder table, we break the middle one in two, leaving the smaller piece. We wrap the larger piece in a napkin. This piece of matzah is now called the Afikoman, and will be hidden. However, it must be found, returned to us, and eaten right after dinner, or the Seder cannot proceed.

Cup of Redemption Haggadah

Maggid
TELLING THE STORY OF PASSOVER
"I have remembered my covenant." (Exodus 6:5)

HA LACHMA ANYA
"THE BREAD OF AFFLICTION"

THE LEADER PLACES THE AFIKOMAN ON HIS RIGHT SHOULDER.

LEADER: This is the bread of affliction that our fathers ate in the land of Egypt. Whoever is hungry, let him come and eat; whoever is in need, let him come and join in celebrating Passover. This year we are here, next year may we be in the land of Israel!

THE SEDER PLATE IS REMOVED AT THIS TIME.

MA NISHTANAH
"HOW DIFFERENT" / THE FOUR QUESTIONS
"When your children ask you, 'What does this ceremony mean to you?' then tell them ..." (Exodus 12:26)

LEADER: How different this night is from all other nights!

A TRANSLITERATED VERSION OF MA NISHTANAH APPEARS ON PAGE PAGE 75.

CHILD: How different this night is from all other nights! On all other nights we eat bread or matzah. On this night why do we eat only matzah?

How different this night is from all other nights! On all other nights we eat all kinds of vegetables. On this night why do we eat only bitter herbs?

How different this night is from all other nights! On all other nights we do not dip our vegetables even once. On this night why do we dip them twice?

How different this night is from all other nights! On all other nights we eat our meals sitting or reclining. On this night why do we eat reclining?

THE SEDER PLATE IS RETURNED. THE MATZOT ARE KEPT UNCOVERED.

LEADER: We were slaves to Pharaoh in Egypt, and the LORD, our God, took us out from there with a strong hand and with an outstretched arm. If the Holy One, blessed be He, had not taken our fathers out of Egypt, then we, our children and our children's children would have remained enslaved to Pharaoh in Egypt. Even if all of us were wise, all of us understanding, all of us knowing the Torah, we would still be obligated to discuss the exodus from Egypt; and everyone who discusses the exodus from Egypt at length is praiseworthy.

Blessed is the Omnipresent One. Blessed is He. Blessed is He who has given the Torah to His people, Israel. Blessed is He! The Torah tells us how to respond to the four types of sons: a wise son, a wicked son, a simple son, and one who is unable to ask.

LEADER: What does the wise son say?

PARTICIPANT: "What is the meaning of the testimonies and the statutes and the rules that the LORD our God has commanded you?"[3] Therefore explain to him the Passover offering: that one may not eat anything after eating the Passover sacrifice.[4]

---

3   Deuteronomy 6:20
4   m.Pesachim 10:8

Cup of Redemption Haggadah

LEADER: What does the wicked son say?

PARTICIPANT: "What does this rite mean to you?" [5]—"To you," he says, but not to himself. By excluding himself from the community he has denied the fundamentals of the faith. Therefore, blunt his teeth and tell him: "It is because of what the LORD did for me when I came out of Egypt." [6]—"For me," but not for him. Had he been there, he would not have been redeemed.

LEADER: What does the simple son say?

PARTICIPANT: "What does this mean?" Tell him: "By a strong hand the LORD brought us out of Egypt, from the house of slavery." [7]

LEADER: As for the son who is unable to ask ...

PARTICIPANT: "You shall tell your son on that day, 'It is because of what the Lord did for me when I came out of Egypt.'" [8]

LEADER: In the beginning our fathers served idols; but now the Omnipresent One has brought us close to His service, as it is said:

> And Joshua said to all the people, "Thus says the LORD, the God of Israel, 'Long ago, your fathers lived beyond the Euphrates, Terah, the father of Abraham and of Nahor; and they served other gods. Then I took your father Abraham from beyond the River and led him through all the land of Canaan, and made his offspring many. I gave him Isaac. And to Isaac I gave Jacob and Esau. And I gave Esau the hill country of Seir to possess, but Jacob and his children went down to Egypt.'" (Joshua 24:2-4)

---

5   Exodus 12:26 (NASB)
6   Exodus 13:8
7   Exodus 13:14
8   Exodus 13:8

Then the LORD said to Abram, "Know for certain that your offspring will be sojourners in a land that is not theirs and will be servants there, and they will be afflicted for four hundred years. But I will bring judgment on the nation that they serve, and afterward they shall come out with great possessions. (Genesis 15:13-14)

THE CUPS ARE LIFTED AS A TOAST, AND EVERYONE SAYS THE FOLLOWING WITH JOY.

ALL: It is this that has stood by our fathers and us. For not only one has risen against us to destroy us, but in every generation they rise against us to destroy us. But the holy One, Blessed be He, rescues us from their hand.

THE CUPS ARE SET BACK DOWN.

PARTICIPANT: The Egyptians treated us badly, and they made us suffer, and they put hard work upon us.

LEADER: "Then we cried to the LORD, the God of our fathers, and the LORD heard our voice and saw our affliction, our toil, and our oppression." [9]

PARTICIPANT: "And we cried out to the LORD, the God of our fathers," as it is said: "During those many days the king of Egypt died, and the people of Israel groaned because of their slavery and cried out for help. Their cry for rescue from slavery came up to God." [10]

LEADER: "And the LORD heard our voice" as it said: "And God heard their groaning, and God remembered his covenant with Abraham, with Isaac, and with Jacob." [11]

---

9   Deuteronomy 26:7
10   Exodus 2:23
11   Exodus 2:24

Cup of Redemption Haggadah

PARTICIPANT: The LORD took us out of Egypt with a strong hand and an outstretched arm, and with a great manifestation, and with signs and wonders.

LEADER: We cried out to God for help and God heard our plea, saw our suffering and responded to our oppression. God remembered the Covenant with our ancestors Abraham, Isaac and Jacob.

PARTICIPANT: The LORD took us out of Egypt, not through an angel, not through a seraph and not through a messenger.

LEADER: The Holy One, blessed be He, did it in His glory by Himself! Thus it is said, "For I will pass through the land of Egypt that night, and I will strike all the firstborn in the land of Egypt, both man and beast; and on all the gods of Egypt I will execute judgments: I am the LORD." [12] "I will pass through the land of Egypt."

ALL: I and not an angel.

LEADER: "I will strike all the firstborn in the land of Egypt."

ALL: I and not a seraph.

LEADER: "On all the gods of Egypt I will execute judgments."

ALL: I and not a messenger.

LEADER: "I am the LORD."

ALL: It is I, and none other!

LEADER: "And the LORD brought us out of Egypt with a mighty hand and an outstretched arm, with great deeds of terror, with signs and wonders." [13]

---

12   Exodus 12:12
13   Deuteronomy 26:8

PARTICIPANT: "With a mighty hand," this refers to the pestilence as it is said: "Behold, the hand of the LORD will fall with a very severe plague upon your livestock that are in the field, the horses, the donkeys, the camels, the herds, and the flocks." [14]

PARTICIPANT: "And an outstretched arm," this refers to the sword, as it is said: "In his hand a drawn sword stretched out over Jerusalem." [15]

PARTICIPANT: "With great deeds of terror," this refers to the revelation of the Shechinah (Divine Presence), as it is said: "Has any god ever attempted to go and take a nation for himself from the midst of another nation, by trials, by signs, by wonders, and by war, by a mighty hand and an outstretched arm, and by great deeds of terror, all of which the LORD your God did for you in Egypt before your eyes?!" [16]

PARTICIPANT: "With signs," this refers to the staff, as it is said: "Take in your hand this staff, with which you shall do the signs." [17]

PARTICIPANT: "And wonders," this refers to the blood, as it is said: "And I will show wonders in the heavens and on the earth , blood and fire and columns of smoke." [18]

---

14   Exodus 9:3
15   1 Chronicles 21:16
16   Deuteronomy 4:34
17   Exodus 4:17
18   Joel 2:30

THE TEN JUDGMENTS

LEADER: These are the Ten Plagues which the Holy One, blessed be He, brought upon the Egyptians.

LEADER READS HEBREW, THEN ENGLISH IS SAID BY ALL THREE TIMES. BEFORE EACH PLAGUE, DIP A FINGER OF THE RIGHT HAND INTO THE CUP. SLING WINE ONTO A NAPKIN AS EACH PLAGUE IS SAID IN ENGLISH EACH TIME.

דָּם	Dom	**Blood!**
צְפַרְדֵּעַ	Tz'fardei-ah	**Frogs!**
כִּנִּים	Kinim	**Lice!**
עָרוֹב	Arov	**Swarms!**
דֶּבֶר	Dever	**Pestilence!**
שְׁחִין	Sh'chin	**Boils!**
בָּרָד	Barad	**Hail!**
אַרְבֶּה	Arbeh	**Locust!**
חֹשֶׁךְ	Choshech	**Darkness!**
מַכַּת בְּכוֹרוֹת	Makat B'chorot	**Death of the Firstborn!**

LEADER: Blessed is He who keeps His promise to Israel, blessed be He! For the Holy One, blessed be He, calculated the end of the bondage, in order to do as He had said to our father Abraham at the "Covenant between the Portions," as it is said: "Then the LORD said to Abram, 'Know for certain that your offspring will be sojourners in a land that is not theirs and will be servants there, and they will be afflicted for four hundred years. But I will bring judgment on the nation that they serve, and afterward they shall come out with great possessions.' "[19]

---

19   Genesis 15:13-14

DAYENU

IT WOULD HAVE BEEN SUFFICIENT

"They shall pour forth the fame of your abundant goodness and
shall sing aloud of your righteousness." (Psalm 145:7)

LEADER: Let us bless the Name of the LORD! How great is God's goodness to
us! For each of His acts of mercy and kindness we declare "Dayenu!"—"it would
have been sufficient."

*If the LORD had merely rescued us, but had
not cast judgment upon the Egyptians...*   דַּיֵּנוּ DAYENU!

*If He had merely cast judgment upon the
Egyptians, but not upon their gods...*   דַּיֵּנוּ DAYENU!

*If He had merely cast judgment upon their
gods, but had not slain their firstborn...*   דַּיֵּנוּ DAYENU!

*If He had merely slain their firstborn,
but had not given us their wealth...*   דַּיֵּנוּ DAYENU!

*If He had merely given us their wealth,
but had not parted the Sea...*   דַּיֵּנוּ DAYENU!

*If He had merely parted the Sea, but
not led us through on dry ground...*   דַּיֵּנוּ DAYENU!

*If He had merely led us through on
dry ground, but had not drowned
our enemies in the waters...*   דַּיֵּנוּ DAYENU!

*If He had merely drowned our
enemies, but had not provided for
us in the desert for forty years...*   דַּיֵּנוּ DAYENU!

Cup of Redemption Haggadah

If He had merely provided for us in the desert, but had not fed us with manna... דַּיֵּנוּ DAYENU!

If He had merely fed us with manna, but had not given us the Sabbath... דַּיֵּנוּ DAYENU!

If He had merely given us the Sabbath, but not brought us to Sinai... דַּיֵּנוּ DAYENU!

If He had merely brought us to Sinai, but not given us His Torah... דַּיֵּנוּ DAYENU!

If He had only given us His Torah, but not led us into the land of Israel... דַּיֵּנוּ DAYENU!

If He had only led us into the land of Israel, but not built the Holy Temple for us... דַּיֵּנוּ DAYENU!

If He had only built the Holy Temple for us, but not given us Messiah, the Torah made flesh... דַּיֵּנוּ DAYENU!

But the Holy One, blessed be He, provided all of these blessings for us. And not only these, but so many more. Blessed are You, O LORD, for You have, in mercy, supplied all our needs. You have given us Messiah Yeshua, and He is sufficient! דַּיֵּנוּ DAYENU!

MATZAH, MAROR, PESACH

"The blood shall be a sign for you, on the houses where you are. And when I see the blood, I will pass over you." (Exodus 12:13)

LEADER: The z'roa (shank bone) represents the paschal lamb offered up at this feast. In the Passover Lamb, we see our Messiah.

PARTICIPANT: "On the tenth day of this month every man shall take a lamb according to their fathers' houses, a lamb for a household ... Your lamb shall be without blemish, a male a year old ... and you shall keep it until the fourteenth day of this month, when the whole assembly of the congregation of Israel shall kill their lambs at twilight. Then they shall take some of the blood and put it on the two doorposts and the lintel of the houses in which they eat it." [20]

PARTICIPANT: On the tenth of Nisan, Yeshua made his famous entry into Jerusalem, riding upon a donkey, at which time he was scrutinized by those in authority. Then, just a few days later, he was slain as our Passover Lamb in order he might take on the sins of the world.

PARTICIPANT: "They shall eat the flesh that night, roasted on the fire; with unleavened bread and bitter herbs they shall eat it ... In this manner you shall eat it: with your belt fastened, your sandals on your feet, and your staff in your hand. And you shall eat it in haste. It is the LORD's Passover ... The blood shall be a sign for you, on the houses where you are. And when I see the blood, I will pass over you, and no plague will befall you to destroy you, when I strike the land of Egypt." [21]

ALL: **We who have trusted Messiah Yeshua as the Lamb of God, apply the blood of the Lamb to the door of our hearts in keeping with obedience that God's judgment may pass over us.**

PARTICIPANT: "You may not offer the Passover sacrifice within any of your towns that the LORD your God is giving you, but at the place that the LORD your God will choose, to make his name dwell in it, there you shall offer the Passover sacrifice" [22]

---

20   Exodus 12:3,5-7
21   Exodus 12:8,11,13
22   Deuteronomy 16:5-6

Cup of Redemption Haggadah

LEADER: Since the Temple in Jerusalem no longer stands, animal sacrifices cannot be made. The Temple Mount is the only acceptable location for sacrifices, especially the Passover offering. Therefore, lamb is not eaten at Passover. This shank bone remains to remind us of both the paschal lamb and our Messiah, the Lamb of God.

LIFT THE MATZAH.

LEADER: This Matzah that we eat is for what reason? Because the dough of our fathers did not have time to become leavened before the King of the kings of kings, the Holy One, blessed be He, revealed Himself to us and redeemed us.

PARTICIPANT: "They baked unleavened cakes of the dough that they had brought out of Egypt, for it was not leavened, because they were thrust out of Egypt and could not wait, nor had they prepared any provisions for themselves." [23]

LIFT THE MAROR.

LEADER: This maror that we eat is for what reason? Because the Egyptians embittered our fathers' lives in Egypt, as it is said: "[They] made their lives bitter with hard service, in mortar and brick, and in all kinds of work in the field. In all their work they ruthlessly made them work as slaves." [24]

In every generation a person is obligated to regard himself as if he had come out of Egypt, as it is said: "You shall tell your son on that day, 'It is because of what the LORD did for me when I came out of Egypt.'" [25]

---

23   Exodus 12:39
24   Exodus 1:14
25   Exodus 13:8

The Holy One, blessed be He, redeemed not only our fathers from Egypt, but He also redeemed us with them, as it is said: "And he brought us out from there, that he might bring us in and give us the land that he swore to give to our fathers."[26]

ALL: "Praise the LORD! Praise, O servants of the LORD, praise the name of the LORD! Blessed be the name of the LORD from this time forth and forevermore! From the rising of the sun to its setting, the name of the LORD is to be praised! The LORD is high above all nations, and his glory above the heavens! Who is like the LORD our God, who is seated on high, who looks far down on the heavens and the earth? He raises the poor from the dust and lifts the needy from the ash heap, to make them sit with princes, with the princes of his people. He gives the barren woman a home, making her the joyous mother of children. Praise the LORD!" (Psalm 113)

ALL: "When Israel went out from Egypt, the house of Jacob from a people of strange language, Judah became his sanctuary, Israel his dominion. The sea looked and fled; Jordan turned back. The mountains skipped like rams, the hills like lambs. What ails you, O sea, that you flee? O Jordan, that you turn back? O mountains, that you skip like rams? O hills, like lambs? Tremble, O earth, at the presence of the Lord, at the presence of the God of Jacob, who turns the rock into a pool of water, the flint into a spring of water." (Psalm 114)

LEADER: Blessed are You, LORD, our God, King of the universe, who has redeemed us and redeemed our fathers from Egypt, and enabled us to attain this night to eat matzah and maror. So too, LORD, our God and God of our fathers, enable us to attain other holidays and festivals that will come to us in peace with happiness in the rebuilding of Your city, and with rejoicing in Your service. Then we shall eat of the sacrifices and of the Passover offerings and we shall thank You with a new song for our redemption and for the deliverance of our souls. Blessed are You, LORD, who redeemed Israel.

---

26   Deuteronomy 6:23

PARTICIPANT: God brought us out of Egypt with all the plunder we could carry. The LORD went ahead of us in a pillar of cloud by day and a pillar of fire by night. But God hardened Pharaoh's heart once more. As we reached the Sea of Reeds, we looked back to see Pharaoh and his army pursuing us. We cried out to the LORD and He delivered us!

PARTICIPANT: We went through the sea on dry ground, with a wall of water on our right and on our left. That day the LORD saved us from the hands of the Egyptians. When the we saw the great power God displayed against the Egyptians, we feared the LORD and put our trust in Him.[27]

LEADER: We see that those who curse or abuse God's people are punished in kind. God cursed the Egyptians in the same manner that the Egyptians had cursed the Hebrews. He killed their firstborn sons and drowned their army, just as the Egyptians had drowned the Hebrew boys in the Nile. Genesis 12:3 states, "I will bless those who bless you, and him who dishonors you I will curse."

Let us always remember that although "a partial hardening has come upon Israel, until the fullness of the Gentiles has come in," [28] they have not been forgotten, replaced, nor disowned. God's gifts and calling are "irrevocable," [29] and the destinies of the Jews and the God-fearing Gentiles who submit to the God of Israel through Messiah Yeshua are forever intertwined, and a mystery.

PARTICIPANT: "When you read this, you can perceive my insight into the mystery of Christ, which was not made known to the sons of men in other generations as it has now been revealed to his holy apostles and prophets by the Spirit. This mystery is that the Gentiles are fellow heirs, members of the same body, and partakers of the promise in Christ Jesus through the gospel." [30]

---

27   Exodus 14:29-31
28   Romans 11:25
29   Romans 11:29
30   Ephesians 3:4-6

Cup of Judgment

"I will deliver you from slavery" (Exodus 6:6)

LEADER: This cup is a symbol of bitterness as well as joy: bitterness because of God's judgment poured out on Pharaoh and the Egyptians, joy because of God's judgment on our behalf, delivering us from a life of slavery.

The Midrash[31] relates that when the Egyptians were drowning in the Sea of Reeds, the angels wished to join in Israel's song of victory by singing "Halleluyah," but God rebuked them, saying: "How can you sing Halleluyah when My creatures are drowning?" In this spirit, we have reduced our second cup of wine by splashing wine out of it. Our gladness is diminished by any human suffering— even the suffering of our enemies.

ALL: "I will deliver you from slavery!" [32]

LEADER: For Messiah Yeshua it was a bitter-sweet cup as well. Knowing that in order for us to be free, he drank the Cup of Judgment on our behalf.

PARTICIPANT: "Father, if you are willing, remove this cup from me. Nevertheless, not my will, but yours, be done." [33]

LEADER: Now let us lift our cups and drink, thanking God that He not only judged the Egyptians, but that through Yeshua, he delivers us from the plagues of sin and death.

---

31   An ancient Jewish commentary on the Scriptures
32   Exodus 6:6
33   Luke 22:42

ALL LIFT CUP WITH RIGHT HAND.

We thank You, our Father, for the holy vine of Your servant
David, that You made known to us through Your servant
Yeshua. To You be the glory forever. (Didache 9:2)

בָּרוּךְ אַתָּה ה'
אֱלֹהֵינוּ מֶלֶךְ
הָעוֹלָם בּוֹרֵא
פְּרִי הַגָּפֶן.

Baruch ata Adonai

Eloheinu Melech

HaOlam borei

p'ri hagafen.

Blessed are You, O
LORD our God, King
of the Universe,
Who creates the
fruit of the vine.

LEAN TO THE LEFT WHILE DRINKING THE CUP OF WINE.

Rachtzah

WASHING THE HANDS FOR THE MEAL

"When they come near the altar to minister ... they shall wash with water." (Exodus 30:20)

For concerns about ritual hand washing, see "Ritual Hand Washing" on page 89. Non-Jewish disciples of Yeshua may forego this blessing. Water is poured over each hand three times, beginning with the right hand.

בָּרוּךְ אַתָּה ה'
אֱלֹהֵינוּ מֶלֶךְ הָעוֹלָם
אֲשֶׁר קִדְּשָׁנוּ
בְּמִצְוֹתָיו וְצִוָּנוּ עַל
נְטִילַת יָדַיִם.

Baruch ata Adonai

Eloheinu Melech

HaOlam asher kidshanu

b'mitzvotav v'tzivanu

al netilat yadayim.

Blessed are You, O LORD
our God, King of the
Universe, Who sanctified us
with Your commandments,
and commanded us
to wash our hands.

Motzi
BLESSING FOR THE BREAD/MATZAH
"I am the bread of life." (John 6:48)

REMOVE ALL THREE MATZOT FROM THE MATZAH TASH AND RAISE THEM TOGETHER.

We thank You, our Father, for the life and knowledge that You made known to us through Your servant Yeshua. To You be the glory forever.

Just as this broken bread was scattered over the hills, and was gathered together and became one, so let Your Congregation be gathered together from the ends of the earth into Your Kingdom; for Yours is the glory and the power through Messiah Yeshua forever. (Didache 9:1–5)

בָּרוּךְ אַתָּה ה'	*Baruch ata Adonai*	Blessed are You, O LORD
אֱלֹהֵינוּ מֶלֶךְ	*Eloheinu Melech*	our God, King of the
הָעוֹלָם הַמּוֹצִיא	*HaOlam hamotzi*	Universe, Who brings forth
לֶחֶם מִן הָאָרֶץ.	*lechem min ha-aretz.*	bread from the earth.

Matzah
BLESSING FOR THE EATING OF MATZAH
"Seven days you shall eat unleavened bread." (Exodus 12:15)

THE BOTTOM MATZAH IS PUT DOWN, AND THE OTHER TWO PIECES ARE RAISED.

LEADER: On all other nights we eat chametz (bread with leaven), but on Passover we eat only matzah, unleavened bread, because the dough had not yet risen when the King of Kings of Kings, the Holy One Blessed be He, revealed Himself to our forefathers in Egypt, and redeemed them.

PARTICIPANT: "And they baked unleavened cakes of the dough that they had brought out of Egypt, for it was not leavened, because they were thrust out of Egypt and could not wait, nor had they prepared any provisions for themselves."[34]

LIFT MATZAH

בְּרוּךְ אַתָּה ה'
אֱלֹהֵינוּ מֶלֶךְ הָעוֹלָם
אֲשֶׁר קִדְּשָׁנוּ
בְּמִצְוֹתָיו וְצִוָּנוּ עַל
אֲכִילַת מַצָּה.

Baruch ata Adonai
Eloheinu Melech
HaOlam asher kidshanu
b'mitzvotav v'tzivanu
al achilat matzah.

Blessed are You, O LORD our God, King of the Universe, Who has sanctified us with His commandments, and has commanded us regarding the eating of the matzah.

THE TOP TWO MATZOT ARE BROKEN AND PASSED.

EAT THE MATZAH WHILE LEANING TO THE LEFT.

---

34   Exodus 12:39

Maror
THE BITTER HERB

"With ... bitter herbs they shall eat it." (Exodus 12:8)

LEADER: On all other nights we eat all kinds of vegetables, but on Passover we eat only maror, bitter herbs. Let us remember how bitter life was for us when we were in the land of Egypt, and never allow the trials and heartaches of life to become hopeless. Tonight we eat bitterness, rather than becoming embittered.

PARTICIPANT: "And the Egyptians were in dread of the people of Israel. So they ruthlessly made the people of Israel work as slaves and made their lives bitter with hard service, in mortar and brick, and in all kinds of work in the field." [35]

LEADER: Our Messiah also suffered bitterness on our behalf, the bitterness of betrayal:

PARTICIPANT: "After saying these things, Jesus was troubled in his spirit, and testified, 'Truly, truly, I say to you, one of you will betray me.' The disciples looked at one another, uncertain of whom he spoke. One of his disciples, whom Jesus loved, was reclining at table at Jesus' side, so Simon Peter motioned to him to ask Jesus of whom he was speaking. So that disciple, leaning back against Jesus, said to him, 'Lord, who is it?' Jesus answered, 'It is he to whom I will give this

---

35   Exodus 1:12–14

Cup of Redemption Haggadah

morsel of bread when I have dipped it.' So when he had dipped the morsel, he gave it to Judas, the son of Simon Iscariot." [36]

PARTICIPANT: Yeshua did not respond with bitterness, but made sure he instilled the value of love into his disciples, saying, "A new commandment I give to you, that you love one another: just as I have loved you, you also are to love one another. By this all people will know that you are my disciples, if you have love for one another." [37]

LEADER: We dip the bitter herbs into charoset to remind ourselves that even the most bitter of circumstances can be sweetened by the hope of redemption. As we eat the maror, let us allow the bitter taste to cause us to shed some tears of compassion for all who suffer the bitterness of this world. May our love for our fellowman absorb the bitterness of this harsh life just as our Master Yeshua did in his final days on this earth.

ALL: Messiah said, "Come to me, all who labor and are heavy laden, and I will give you rest." [38]

TAKE SOME MAROR AND PLACE IT ONTO A SMALL PIECE OF MATZAH. DIP THE MATZAH AND MAROR INTO THE CHAROSET, BUT SHAKE OFF MOST OF THE CHAROSET. LIFT THE MATZAH AND MAROR WITH THE RIGHT HAND AND RECITE THIS BLESSING.

בָּרוּךְ אַתָּה ה' אֱלֹהֵינוּ מֶלֶךְ הָעוֹלָם אֲשֶׁר קִדְּשָׁנוּ בְּמִצְוֹתָיו וְצִוָּנוּ עַל אֲכִילַת מָרוֹר.	*Baruch ata Adonai Eloheinu Melech HaOlam asher kidshanu b'mitzvotav v'tzivanu al achilat maror.*	**Blessed are You, O LORD our God, King of the Universe, Who sanctified us with Your commandments, and commanded us to eat the bitter herb.**

EAT THE MATZAH AND MAROR WHILE LEANING TO THE LEFT.

---

36 John 13:21–26
37 John 13:34–35
38 Matthew 11:28

Korech
EATING OF THE HILLEL SANDWICH

"With unleavened bread and bitter herbs they shall eat it." (Exodus 12:8)

THE LEADER DIVIDES AND PASSES THE BOTTOM PIECE OF MATZAH FOR THE PARTICIPANTS TO USE IN THE HILLEL SANDWICH. EACH PARTICIPANT WILL SUPPLEMENT WITH ADDITIONAL MATZAH AND PLACE SOME OF THE CHAZARET AND THE CHAROSET BETWEEN THE TWO PIECES OF MATZAH. AS SOON AS YOU HAVE MADE THE SANDWICH, EAT IT IMMEDIATELY WITHOUT LEANING.

LEADER: We toiled to make treasure cities for Pharaoh, working in brick and clay. We remember this task in a mixture called charoset, made from chopped apples, honey, nuts, and wine. It symbolizes the mortar that our ancestors used to build the pyramids. The sweet taste reminds us that even in the most bitter depths of slavery our ancestors never stopped yearning for the sweet taste of freedom. It is also a reminder of how the sweetness of Messiah Yeshua's resurrection gives us the ability to overcome the bitter curse of sin in our lives. In eating the Hillel Sandwich we let it linger in our mouths, for it is only when we remember the degradation of where we came from that we can truly appreciate where we are today.

Shulchan Orech
FESTIVAL MEAL ("SETTING THE TABLE")

"You shall keep it as a feast to the LORD; throughout your generations,
as a statute forever, you shall keep it as a feast." (Exodus 12:14)

REMOVE THE SEDER PLATE. SERVE THE FESTIVE MEAL.

—DISCREETLY HIDE AFIKOMAN—

*AT THE CONCLUSION OF THE MEAL, POUR THE THIRD CUP
OF WINE AND CONTINUE WITH TZAFUN.*

Tzafun
"HIDDEN" / EATING THE AFIKOMAN

"He was cut off out of the land of the living, stricken for the
transgression of my people." (Isaiah 53:8)

**RETURN SEDER PLATE. CHILDREN SEARCH FOR THE AFIKOMAN. LEADER
"RANSOMS" THE AFIKOMAN WITH A REWARD FOR THE CHILD WHO FOUND IT.**

LEADER: The Afikoman, the dessert, is the final food eaten at Passover. In sharing the Afikoman, we share in the suffering of our Messiah. In the stripes of the matzah we see a picture of Yeshua our Master.

PARTICIPANT: "Then Pilate took Jesus and flogged him." [39]

ALL: **"But he was pierced for our transgressions; he was crushed for our iniquities; upon him was the chastisement that brought us peace, and with his wounds we are healed."** [40]

LEADER: And just as the matzah is pierced, so too was our Messiah.

PARTICIPANT: "And when they came to the place that is called The Skull, there they crucified him, and the criminals, one on his right and one on his left." [41]

---

39 John 19:1
40 Isaiah 53:5
41 Luke 23:33

Cup of Redemption Haggadah

PARTICIPANT: "And the people stood by, watching, but the rulers scoffed at him, saying, 'He saved others; let him save himself, if he is the Christ of God, his Chosen One!' The soldiers also mocked him, coming up and offering him sour wine and saying, 'If you are the King of the Jews, save yourself!'" [42]

ALL: "And I will pour out on the house of David and the inhabitants of Jerusalem a spirit of grace and pleas for mercy, so that, when they look on me, on him whom they have pierced, they shall mourn for him, as one mourns for an only child, and weep bitterly over him, as one weeps over a firstborn." [43]

PARTICIPANT: "And about the ninth hour Jesus cried out with a loud voice, saying, 'Eli, Eli, lema sabachthani?' that is, 'My God, my God, why have you forsaken me?'" [44]

PARTICIPANT: "Then Jesus, calling out with a loud voice, said, 'Father, into your hands I commit my spirit!'" [45]

PARTICIPANT: "He said, 'It is finished,' and he bowed his head and gave up his spirit.'" [46]

PARTICIPANT: "Since it was the day of Preparation, and so that the bodies would not remain on the cross on the Sabbath (for that Sabbath was a high day), the Jews asked Pilate that their legs might be broken and that they might be taken away. So the soldiers came and broke the legs of the first, and of the other who had been crucified with him. But when they came to Jesus and saw that he was already dead, they did not break his legs. But one of the soldiers pierced his side with a spear, and at once there came out blood and water. He who saw it has borne witness—his testimony is true, and he knows that he is telling the truth—that you also may believe. For these things took place that

---

42   Luke 23:35–37
43   Zechariah 12:10
44   Matthew 27:46 (quoting Psalm 22:1)
45   Luke 23:46
46   John 19:30

the Scripture might be fulfilled: 'Not one of his bones will be broken.' And again another Scripture says, 'They will look on him whom they have pierced.'" [47]

LEADER: Just as the middle piece of matzah was broken and became the bread of affliction, Messiah, too, was afflicted and broken.

ALL: **"I have been forgotten like one who is dead; I have become like a broken vessel."** [48]

LEADER: Just as the matzah is without yeast, Yeshua was without sin. The one born in Bethlehem ("House of Bread") now provides the "bread of life" to all who partake of Him.

LEADER: Remember how the Afikoman was wrapped in a cloth? In the same manner Messiah's body was wrapped for burial.

PARTICIPANT: "So they took the body of Jesus and bound it in linen cloths with the spices, as is the burial custom of the Jews. Now in the place where he was crucified there was a garden, and in the garden a new tomb in which no one had yet been laid. So because of the Jewish day of Preparation, since the tomb was close at hand, they laid Jesus there." [49]

LEADER: Then the Afikoman was hidden—as Messiah was placed in a tomb— hidden for a time. But just as the Afikoman returned to complete our Passover seder, so the sinless Messiah rose from the dead, being the Firstfruit of the resurrection of the faithful.

BREAK AND PASS THE AFIKOMAN TO ALL IN SILENCE. DO NOT EAT AT THIS TIME.

---

47   John 19:31–37 (quoting Psalm 34:20 and Zechariah 12:10)
48   Psalm 31:12
49   John 19:41–42

Cup of Redemption Haggadah

LEADER: Just as our Messiah was without the leaven of sin, may we cast out the leaven of sin in our own lives, faithfully abiding in his love.

PARTICIPANT: "Do you not know that a little leaven leavens the whole lump? Cleanse out the old leaven that you may be a new lump, as you really are unleavened. For Christ, our Passover lamb, has been sacrificed. Let us therefore celebrate the festival, not with the old leaven, the leaven of malice and evil, but with the unleavened bread of sincerity and truth." [50]

PARTICIPANT: "Whoever, therefore, eats the bread or drinks the cup of the Lord in an unworthy manner will be guilty concerning the body and blood of the Lord. Let a person examine himself, then, and so eat of the bread and drink of the cup. For anyone who eats and drinks without discerning the body eats and drinks judgment on himself." [51]

LEADER: It is in this season that we search ourselves, examining our hearts for anything that might be an offense to our God. Just as chametz easily permeates a batch of dough, so sin permeates our lives if left unattended. Tonight let us be like King David when he said: "Search me, O God, and know my heart! Try me and know my thoughts! And see if there be any grievous way in me, and lead me in the way everlasting!" [52] As we break matzah, let us pause to examine ourselves in order that we may not eat of the Lord's bread in an unworthy manner.

PARTICIPANT: "And he took bread, and when he had given thanks, he broke it and gave it to them, saying, 'This is my body, which is given for you. Do this in remembrance of me.'" [53]

LEADER: As we partake of the Afikoman, let us meditate on the broken body of Yeshua our Messiah.

---

50   1 Corinthians 5:6b-8
51   1 Corinthians 11:27–29
52   Psalm 139:23–24
53   Luke 22:19

LIFT MATZAH WITH RIGHT HAND.

ALL: Blessed is the Lamb of God, who takes away the sin of the world!

We thank You, our Father, for the life and knowledge that You made known
to us through Your servant Yeshua. To You be the glory forever.

Just as this broken bread was scattered over the hills, and was gathered
together and became one, so let Your Congregation be gathered together
from the ends of the earth into Your Kingdom; for Yours is the glory and
the power through Messiah Yeshua forever. (Didache 9:1–5)

בָּרוּךְ אַתָּה ה'	*Baruch ata Adonai*	Blessed are You, O LORD
אֱלֹהֵינוּ מֶלֶךְ	*Eloheinu Melech*	our God, King of the
הָעוֹלָם הַמּוֹצִיא	*HaOlam hamotzi*	Universe, Who brings forth
לֶחֶם מִן הָאָרֶץ.	*lechem min ha-aretz.*	bread from the earth.

EAT THE AFIKOMAN WHILE LEANING TO THE LEFT.

LEADER: Now, except for the two remaining cups of wine, no food may be
eaten after the Afikoman.

Barech
GRACE AFTER MEALS

"You shall eat and be full, and you shall bless the LORD your God." (Deuteronomy 8:10)

**ALL THE TEXT OF GRACE AFTER MEALS SHOULD BE RECITED BY
ALL PARTICIPANTS UNLESS OTHERWISE NOTED.**

✿ PSALM 126 ✿

A Song of Ascents. When the LORD restored the fortunes of Zion, we were like those who dream. Then our mouth was filled with laughter, and our tongue with shouts of joy; then they said among the nations, "The LORD has done great things for them." The LORD has done great things for us; we are glad. Restore our fortunes, O LORD, like streams in the Negeb! Those who sow in tears shall reap with shouts of joy! He who goes out weeping, bearing the seed for sowing, shall come home with shouts of joy, bringing his sheaves with him.

If three or more males thirteen years old or older are present, include the following. If ten or more males thirteen years old or older are present, include the words in brackets.

LEADER: Gentlemen, let us bless.

PARTICIPANTS: May the Name of the LORD be blessed from now and forever.[54]

LEADER: With the permission of our gentlemen and our teachers and my masters, let us bless [our God] from whom we have eaten.

PARTICIPANTS: Blessed is [our God] from whom we have eaten and from whose goodness we live.

---

54   Psalms 113:2

LEADER: Blessed is [our God] from whom we have eaten and from whose goodness we live.

❧ BLESSING FOR THE FOOD ❧

DIDACHE
BLESSING
We thank You, holy Father, for Your holy name that You caused to dwell in our hearts, and for the knowledge and faith and immortality, that You made known to us through Your servant Yeshua. To You be the glory forever.[55]

Blessed are You, LORD our God, King of the Universe, who nourishes the entire world in His goodness, in grace, in kindness and in mercy; He gives bread to all flesh since His kindness is forever. And in His great goodness, we have never lacked, and may we never lack nourishment forever and always, because of His great name. Since He is a Power that feeds and provides for all and does good to all and prepares nourishment for all of his creatures that he created. Blessed are You, LORD, who sustains all.

❧ BLESSING FOR THE LAND ❧

DIDACHE
BLESSING
You, Almighty Master, created all things for Your name's sake. You gave food and drink to all men for enjoyment, that they might give thanks to You. But to us You freely gave spiritual food and drink and eternal life through Your Servant. Above all, we thank You because You are powerful. To You be the glory forever.[56]

We thank you, LORD our God, that you have given as an inheritance to our ancestors a lovely, good and broad land, and that You took us out, Lord our God, from the land of Egypt and that You redeemed us from a house of slaves,

---

55   Didache 10:2
56   Didache 10:3–4

Cup of Redemption Haggadah

and for Your covenant which You have sealed in our flesh,[57] and for Your Torah that You have taught us, and for Your statutes which You have made known to us, and for life, grace and kindness that You have granted us and for the eating of nourishment that You feed and provide for us always, on all days, and at all times and in every hour.

And for everything, LORD our God, we thank You and bless You; may Your name be blessed by the mouth of all life, constantly forever and always, as it is written, "And you shall eat and you shall be satiated and you shall bless the LORD your God for the good land that He has given you." [58] Blessed are You, LORD, for the land and for the nourishment.

✼ BLESSING FOR JERUSALEM ✼

DIDACHE BLESSING

Remember, O LORD, Your Congregation, to deliver it from all evil and to perfect it in Your love. Gather it together, Your sanctified one, from the four winds into Your Kingdom that You have prepared for it. For Yours is the power and the glory forever.[59]

Please have mercy, LORD our God, upon Israel, Your people; and upon Jerusalem, Your city; and upon Zion, the dwelling place of Your Glory; and upon the monarchy of the House of David, Your anointed one; and upon the great and holy house that Your name is called upon. Our God, our Father, tend us, sustain us, provide for us, relieve us and give us quick relief, LORD our God, from all of our troubles. And please do not make us needy, LORD our God, not for the gifts of flesh and blood, and not for their loans, but rather from Your full, open, holy and broad hand, so that we not be embarrassed and we not be ashamed forever and always.

---

57 *"which You have sealed in our flesh"*—Gentiles should say "which You have sealed with our father Abraham ... "
58 Deuteronomy 8:10
59 Didache 10:5

ON SABBATH ADD THIS PARAGRAPH.

[May You be pleased to embolden us, LORD our God, in your commandments and in the command of the seventh day, of this great and holy Shabbat, since this day is great and holy before You, to cease work upon it and to rest upon it, with love, according to the commandment of Your will. And with Your will, allow us, LORD our God, that we should not have trouble, and grief and sighing on the day of our rest. And may You show us, LORD our God, the consolation of Zion, Your city; and the building of Jerusalem, Your holy city; since You are the Master of salvations and the Master of consolations.]

BLESSING FOR THE FESTIVAL

God and God of our ancestors, may there ascend and come and reach and be seen and be acceptable and be heard and be recalled and be remembered - our remembrance and our recollection; and the remembrance of our ancestors; and the remembrance of the messiah, the son of David, Your servant; and the remembrance of Jerusalem, Your holy city; and the remembrance of all Your people, the house of Israel - in front of You, for survival, for good, for grace, and for kindness, and for mercy, for life and for peace on this day of the Festival of Matzot. Remember us, LORD our God, on it for good and recall us on it for survival and save us on it for life, and by the word of salvation and mercy, pity and grace us and have mercy on us and save us, since our eyes are upon You, since You are a graceful and merciful Power. And may You build Jerusalem, the holy city, quickly and in our days. Blessed are You, LORD, who builds Jerusalem in His mercy. Amen.

BLESSING FOR GOD'S GOODNESS

Blessed are You, LORD our God, King of the Universe, the Power, our Father, our King, our Mighty One, our Creator, our Redeemer, our Shaper, our Holy One, the Holy One of Jacob, our Shepherd, the Shepherd of Israel, the good King, who does good to all, since on every single day He has done good, He does good, He will do good, to us; He has granted us, He grants us, He will grant us forever - in grace and in kindness, and in mercy, and in relief - rescue and success, blessing and salvation, consolation, provision and relief and mercy and life and peace and all good; and may we not lack any good ever.

May the Compassionate One reign over us forever and always.

May the Compassionate One be blessed in the heavens and in the earth.

May the Compassionate One be praised for all generations, and exalted among us forever and ever, and glorified among us always and infinitely for all infinities.

May the Compassionate One sustain us honorably.

May the Compassionate One break our yoke from upon our necks and bring us upright to our land.

May the Compassionate One send us multiple blessing, to this home and upon this table upon which we have eaten.

May the Compassionate One send us Eliyahu the prophet—may he be remembered for good - and he shall announce to us tidings of good, of salvation and of consolation.

ADD THE WORDS IN BRACKETS IF APPROPRIATE.

LEADER: May the Compassionate One bless me [my wife/my husband/my children] and all that is mine.

PARTICIPANT: May the Compassionate One bless [my father, my teacher,] the master of this home and [my mother, my teacher,] the lady of this home, them and their home and their offspring and everything that is theirs.

Us and all that is ours; as were blessed Abraham, Isaac, and Jacob, in everything, from everything, with everything, so too should He bless us, all of us together, with a complete blessing and we shall say, Amen. From above, may they advocate upon them and upon us merit, that should protect us in peace; and may we carry a blessing from the LORD and charity from the God of our salvation; and find grace and good understanding in the eyes of God and man.

ON SABBATH ADD THIS PARAGRAPH.

[May the Compassionate One give us to inherit the day that will be completely Shabbat and rest in everlasting life.]

May the Compassionate One give us to inherit the day that will be all good.

ON SABBATH ADD THIS PARAGRAPH.

[The day that is all long, the day that the righteous will sit and their crowns will be on their heads and they will enjoy the radiance of the Divine Presence and my our share be with them.]

May the Compassionate One give us merit for the times of the messiah and for life in the world to come.

A tower of salvations is our King; may He do kindness with his messiah, with David and his offspring, forever.[60] The One who makes peace above, may He make peace upon us and upon all of Israel; and say, Amen. Fear the LORD, His holy ones, since there is no lacking for those that fear Him. Young lions may go without and hunger, but those that seek the LORD will not lack any good thing.[61] Thank the LORD, since He is good, since His kindness is forever.[62] You open Your hand and satisfy the will of all living things.[63] Blessed is the man that trusts in the LORD and the LORD is his security.[64] I was a youth and I have

---

60   II Samuel 22:51
61   Psalms 34:10-11
62   Psalms 118:1
63   Psalms 146:16
64   Jeremiah 17:7

Cup of Redemption Haggadah

also aged and I have not seen a righteous man forsaken and his offspring seeking bread.[65] The LORD will give courage to His people. The LORD will bless His people with peace.[66]

Let grace come, and let this world pass away. Hosanna to the God of David! If any one is holy, let him come; if any one is not, let him repent. Maranatha. Amen.[67]

The Cup of Redemption
"I will redeem you with an outstretched arm" (Exodus 6:6)

LIFT CUP IN RIGHT HAND.

LEADER: This is the cup of redemption, symbolizing the blood of the Passover lamb. It is worth noting that without the LORD's redemption, our deliverance from Egypt would not have been complete. We would have been free from the land of Egypt, but we would still be slaves on the run. It is His redemption that transforms us from slaves into free sons and daughters.

ALL: "I will redeem you with an outstretched arm!"

PARTICIPANT: "Behold, the days are coming, declares the LORD, when I will make a new covenant with the house of Israel and the house of Judah, not like

---

65   Psalms 37:25
66   Psalms 29:11
67   Didache 10:6

the covenant that I made with their fathers on the day when I took them by the hand to bring them out of the land of Egypt, my covenant that they broke, though I was their husband, declares the Lord. For this is the covenant that I will make with the house of Israel after those days, declares the LORD: I will put my law within them, and I will write it on their hearts. And I will be their God, and they shall be my people. And no longer shall each one teach his neighbor and each his brother, saying, 'Know the LORD,' for they shall all know me, from the least of them to the greatest, declares the LORD. For I will forgive their iniquity, and I will remember their sin no more." [68]

LEADER: Messiah Yeshua lifted the cup, saying, "This cup that is poured out for you is the new covenant in my blood." [69]

PARTICIPANT: Just as the blood of the lamb brought salvation in Egypt, so Messiah's atoning death can bring salvation to all who faithfully abide in His covenant of mercy.

LEADER: As we have experienced first-hand the redemption of the LORD tonight by His mighty hand of deliverance, let us not forget those who remain slaves to the Adversary and the Powers of Darkness. Let us never forget to bring justice to the oppressed, freedom to the captive, an out-stretched hand to the poor, the fatherless and the widow, comfort to those who mourn, wine and oil to the broken-hearted, and to always proclaim the Good News to those whom the LORD, our God, would put in our daily path. May Redemption never be a commodity or an exclusive experience. Nor may we ever forget to bring redemption to the realm of the practical, affecting the lives of those around us for the Kingdom of our God in a manner worthy of the name of our Redeemer.

A CHILD OPENS THE FRONT DOOR TO SEARCH FOR ELIJAH.

---

68   Jeremiah 31:31-34
69   Luke 22:20

Cup of Redemption Haggadah

PARTICIPANT: "Behold, I will send you Elijah the prophet before the great and awesome day of the LORD comes. And he will turn the hearts of fathers to their children and the hearts of children to their fathers, lest I come and strike the land with a decree of utter destruction." [70]

SEE SUGGESTED SONGS ON PAGE 77.

ALL LIFT CUP WITH RIGHT HAND.

We thank You, our Father, for the holy vine of Your servant
David, that You made known to us through Your servant
Yeshua. To You be the glory forever. (Didache 9:2)

בָּרוּךְ אַתָּה ה'	*Baruch ata Adonai*	Blessed are You, O
אֱלֹהֵינוּ מֶלֶךְ	*Eloheinu Melech*	LORD our God, King
הָעוֹלָם בּוֹרֵא	*HaOlam borei*	of the Universe, Who creates the
פְּרִי הַגָּפֶן.	*p'ri hagafen.*	fruit of the vine.

LEAN TO THE LEFT WHILE DRINKING THE CUP OF WINE.

THE FOURTH CUP OF WINE IS NOW POURED.

---

70   Malachi 4:5–6

Hallel

PRAISE

*THE HALLEL IS BEGUN BY THE LEADER, AND READ RESPONSIVELY,
WITH THE WORDS IN BOLD READ BY ALL PARTICIPANTS.*

✺ PSALM 115 ✺

Not to us, O LORD, not to us, but to your name give glory,
 for the sake of your steadfast love and your faithfulness!

Why should the nations say,
"Where is their God?"
 Our God is in the heavens;
 he does all that he pleases.

Their idols are silver and gold,
the work of human hands.
 They have mouths, but do not speak;
 eyes, but do not see.
They have ears, but do not hear;
noses, but do not smell.
 They have hands, but do not feel;
 feet, but do not walk;
 and they do not make a sound in their throat.
Those who make them become like them;
so do all who trust in them.

O Israel, trust in the LORD!
 He is their help and their shield.

O house of Aaron, trust in the LORD!
He is their help and their shield.
You who fear the LORD, trust in the LORD!
He is their help and their shield.

The LORD has remembered us;
he will bless us;
he will bless the house of Israel;
he will bless the house of Aaron;
he will bless those who fear the LORD,
both the small and the great.

May the LORD give you increase,
you and your children!
May you be blessed by the LORD,
who made heaven and earth!

The heavens are the LORD's heavens,
but the earth he has given to the children of man.
The dead do not praise the LORD,
nor do any who go down into silence.
But we will bless the LORD
from this time forth and forevermore.
Praise the LORD!

≈ PSALM 116 ≈

I love the LORD, because he has heard
my voice and my pleas for mercy.
Because he inclined his ear to me,
therefore I will call on him as long as I live.
The snares of death encompassed me;
the pangs of Sheol laid hold on me;
I suffered distress and anguish.

Then I called on the name of the LORD:
   "O LORD, I pray, deliver my soul!"

Gracious is the LORD, and righteous;
   our God is merciful.
The LORD preserves the simple;
   when I was brought low, he saved me.
Return, O my soul, to your rest;
   for the LORD has dealt bountifully with you.

For you have delivered my soul from death,
   my eyes from tears,
   my feet from stumbling;
I will walk before the LORD
   in the land of the living.

I believed, even when I spoke:
   "I am greatly afflicted";
I said in my alarm,
   "All mankind are liars."

What shall I render to the LORD
for all his benefits to me?
   I will lift up the cup of salvation
   and call on the name of the LORD,
I will pay my vows to the LORD
in the presence of all his people.

Precious in the sight of the LORD
is the death of his saints.
   O LORD, I am your servant;
   I am your servant, the son of your maidservant.

You have loosed my bonds.
I will offer to you the sacrifice of thanksgiving
and call on the name of the LORD.
I will pay my vows to the LORD
in the presence of all his people,
in the courts of the house of the LORD,
in your midst, O Jerusalem.
Praise the LORD!

⅏ PSALM 117 ⅏

Praise the LORD, all nations!
Extol him, all peoples!
For great is his steadfast love toward us,
and the faithfulness of the LORD endures forever.
Praise the LORD!

⅏ PSALM 118 ⅏

Oh give thanks to the LORD, for he is good;
for his steadfast love endures forever!

Let Israel say,
"His steadfast love endures forever."
Let the house of Aaron say,
"His steadfast love endures forever."
Let those who fear the LORD say,
"His steadfast love endures forever."

Out of my distress I called on the LORD;
the LORD answered me and set me free.
The LORD is on my side; I will not fear.
What can man do to me?
The LORD is on my side as my helper;
I shall look in triumph on those who hate me.

It is better to take refuge in the LORD
than to trust in man.
It is better to take refuge in the LORD
than to trust in princes.

All nations surrounded me;
in the name of the LORD I cut them off!
They surrounded me, surrounded me on every side;
in the name of the LORD I cut them off!
They surrounded me like bees;
they went out like a fire among thorns;
in the name of the LORD I cut them off!
I was pushed hard, so that I was falling,
but the LORD helped me.

The LORD is my strength and my song;
he has become my salvation.
Glad songs of salvation
are in the tents of the righteous:
"The right hand of the LORD does valiantly,
the right hand of the LORD exalts,
the right hand of the LORD does valiantly!"

I shall not die, but I shall live,
and recount the deeds of the LORD.
The LORD has disciplined me severely,
but he has not given me over to death.

Open to me the gates of righteousness,
that I may enter through them
and give thanks to the LORD.
This is the gate of the LORD;
the righteous shall enter through it.

I thank you that you have answered me
   and have become my salvation.
The stone that the builders rejected
   has become the cornerstone.
This is the LORD's doing;
   it is marvelous in our eyes.
This is the day that the LORD has made;
   let us rejoice and be glad in it.

Save us, we pray, O LORD!
   O LORD, we pray, give us success!

Blessed is he who comes in the name of the LORD!
   We bless you from the house of the LORD.
The LORD is God,
   and he has made his light to shine upon us.
Bind the festal sacrifice with cords,
up to the horns of the altar!

You are my God, and I will give thanks to you;
   you are my God; I will extol you.
Oh give thanks to the LORD, for he is good;
   for his steadfast love endures forever!

✺ PSALM 136 ("THE GREAT HALLEL") ✺

Give thanks to the LORD, for he is good,
   for his steadfast love endures forever.
Give thanks to the God of gods,
   for his steadfast love endures forever.
Give thanks to the LORD of lords,
   for his steadfast love endures forever;

to him who alone does great wonders,
   for his steadfast love endures forever;
to him who by understanding made the heavens,
   for his steadfast love endures forever;
to him who spread out the earth above the waters,
   for his steadfast love endures forever;
to him who made the great lights,
   for his steadfast love endures forever;
the sun to rule over the day,
   for his steadfast love endures forever;
the moon and stars to rule over the night,
   for his steadfast love endures forever;

to him who struck down the firstborn of Egypt,
   for his steadfast love endures forever;
and brought Israel out from among them,
   for his steadfast love endures forever;
with a strong hand and an outstretched arm,
   for his steadfast love endures forever;
to him who divided the Red Sea in two,
   for his steadfast love endures forever;
and made Israel pass through the midst of it,
   for his steadfast love endures forever;
but overthrew Pharaoh and his host in the Red Sea,
   for his steadfast love endures forever;
to him who led his people through the wilderness,
   for his steadfast love endures forever;

to him who struck down great kings,
   for his steadfast love endures forever;
and killed mighty kings,
   for his steadfast love endures forever;
Sihon, king of the Amorites,
   for his steadfast love endures forever;

Cup of Redemption Haggadah

and Og, king of Bashan,
   for his steadfast love endures forever;
and gave their land as a heritage,
   for his steadfast love endures forever;
a heritage to Israel his servant,
   for his steadfast love endures forever.

It is he who remembered us in our low estate,
   for his steadfast love endures forever;
and rescued us from our foes,
   for his steadfast love endures forever;
he who gives food to all flesh,
   for his steadfast love endures forever.

Give thanks to the God of heaven,
   for his steadfast love endures forever.

The Cup of the Kingdom

"I will take you to be my people, and I will be your God" (Exodus 6:7)

LEADER: Let us lift our last cup together and bless the Name of our LORD!

ALL LIFT CUP WITH RIGHT HAND.

We thank You, our Father, for the holy vine of Your servant David, that You made known to us through Your servant Yeshua. To You be the glory forever. (Didache 9:2)

בָּרוּךְ אַתָּה ה'	*Baruch ata Adonai*	Blessed are You, O
אֱלֹהֵינוּ מֶלֶךְ	*Eloheinu Melech*	LORD our God, King of the Universe,
הָעוֹלָם בּוֹרֵא	*HaOlam borei*	Who creates the
פְּרִי הַגָּפֶן.	*p'ri hagafen.*	fruit of the vine.

LEAN TO THE LEFT WHILE DRINKING THE CUP OF WINE.

Nirtzah
PRAYER OF ACCEPTANCE

LEADER: "It shall come to pass in the latter days that the mountain of the house of the LORD shall be established as the highest of the mountains, and shall be raised up above the hills; and peoples shall flow to it, and many nations shall come, and say: 'Come, let us go up to the mountain of the LORD, to the house of the God of Jacob; that He may teach us His ways and we may walk in His paths.' For out of Zion shall go forth the Torah, and the word of the LORD from Jerusalem." [71]

The seder of Passover is now completed according to its laws, according to all its ordinances and statutes. Just as we have merited to perform it, so too, may we merit to do it in the future. O Pure One who dwells on high, raise up the congregation that cannot be counted soon. Lead the offshoots of Your sapling, redeemed, to Zion in joy. Then we will sing a new song of thanks, as it is said:

> And they sang a new song, saying, "Worthy are you to take the scroll and to open its seals, for you were slain, and by your blood you ransomed people for God from every tribe and language and people and nation, and you have made them a kingdom and priests to our God, and they shall reign on the earth."[72]

L'SHANAH HABA'A BIRUSHALAYIM!

NEXT YEAR IN JERUSALEM!!!

---

71   Micah 4:1–2
72   Revelation 5:9–10

COUNTING THE OMER

Blessed are You, LORD our God, King of the Universe, Who has sanctified us with His commandments and has commanded us on the counting of the omer. Today is the first day of the omer. The Compassionate One may He return for us the service of the Holy Temple in its place, quickly in our days.

⚘ PSALM 67 ⚘

To the choirmaster: with stringed instruments. A Psalm. A Song.

May God be gracious to us and bless us and make his face to shine upon us, Selah that your way may be known on earth, your saving power among all nations. Let the peoples praise you, O God; let all the peoples praise you!

Let the nations be glad and sing for joy, for you judge the peoples with equity and guide the nations upon earth. Selah Let the peoples praise you, O God; let all the peoples praise you!

The earth has yielded its increase; God, our God, shall bless us. God shall bless us; let all the ends of the earth fear him!

SONGS

SONGS

MA NISHTANAH (HOW DIFFERENT)

Ma Nishtanah halaila hazeh	How different is this night
mikol haleilot? mikol haleilot?	From all nights, from all nights!
Sheh bechol haleilot anu ochlin	On all other nights we eat
chametz umatzah, chametz umatzah.	Bread or matzah, bread or matzah.
Halaila hazeh, halaila hazeh	On this night , on this night
kulo matzah	Only matzah?
Sheh bechol haleilot anu ochlin	On all other nights we eat
she-ar yerakot, she-ar yerakot.	Many vegetables, many vegetables.
Halailah hazeh, halailah hazeh	On this night, on this night
maror, maror	Bitter herb, bitter herb?
Sheh bechol haleilot ein anu matbilin	On all other nights we do not
afilu pa-am echat, afilu pa-am echat.	Dip even once, dip even once.
Halaila hazeh, halaila hazeh	On this night, on this night
shetei pe-a-mim	We dip twice?
Sheh bechol haleilot anu ochlin	On all other nights we eat
bein yoshvin uvein mesubin,	Sitting or reclining,
bein yoshvin uvein mesubin.	Sitting or reclining.
Halaila hazeh, halaila hazeh	On this night, on this night
kulanu mesubin	Only reclining?

DAIYENU (IT WOULD HAVE BEEN SUFFICIENT)

Illu hotzi, hotzianu,	*If He brought, brought us*
Hotzianu mimitzrayim,	*Brought us out of Egypt,*
Hotzianu mimitzrayim,	*Brought us out of Egypt*
Daiyenu!	*It would have been sufficient!*

Dai-dai-yenu ... Daiyenu, Daiyenu!   *It would have been sufficient!*

Illu natan, natan lanu,	*If He had given, given us*
Natan lanu et HaShabbat	*Given us the Sabbath*
Natan lanu et HaShabbat,	*Given us the Sabbath,*
Daiyenu!	*It would have been sufficient!*

Dai-dai-yenu ... Daiyenu, Daiyenu!   *It would have been sufficient!*

Illu natan, natan lanu,	*If He had given, given us*
Natan lanu et HaTorah	*Given us the Torah,*
Natan lanu et HaTorah,	*Given us the Torah,*
Daiyenu!	*It would have been sufficient!*

Dai-dai-yenu ... Daiyenu, Daiyenu!   *It would have been sufficient!*

Illu natan, natan lanu,	*If He had given, given us*
Natan lanu et Mashiach,	*Given us Messiah,*
Natan lanu et Mashiach,	*Given us Messiah,*
Daiyenu!	*It would have been sufficient!*

Dai-dai-yenu ... Daiyenu, Daiyenu!   *It would have been sufficient!*

Cup of Redemption Haggadah

ELIYAHU HANAVI (THE PROPHET ELIJAH)

Eliyahu HaNavi,	Elijah the Prophet,
Eliyahu HaTishbee,	Elijah the Tishbite
Eliyahu Eliyahu,	Elijah, Elijah,
Eliyahu HaGiladee	Elijah the Giliadite
Bimhayra v'yamaynu	Speedily in our days
yavo eilaynu,	may he come to us
Im Mashiach Ben David,	With Messiah, Son of David,
Im Mashiach Ben David	With Messiah, Son of David

ANI MA'AMIN (I BELIEVE)

Ani ma'amin	I believe
B'emuna sheleimah	With complete faith
B'viat HaMashiach	In the coming of The Messiah
Ani ma'amin	I believe

(repeat)

V'af al pi sheyit-ma-meiha	And even though He may tarry
Im kol zeh achakei lo	Nonetheless I will wait for Him
Achakei lo	Wait for Him
B'chol yom shei-yavo	Every day for Him to come
B'chol yom shei-yavo	Every day for Him to come

ECHAD MI YODEA (WHO KNOWS ONE?)

Echad mi yode'a
Echad ani yode'a
Echad Elokeinu shebashamaim
uva'aretz.

Who knows one?
I know one:
One is our God in the heavens and
the earth.

Shnaim mi yode'a
Shnaim ani yode'a
shnei luchot habrit
echad elokeinu shebashamaim
uva'aretz.

Who knows two?
I know two:
Two are the tablets of the covenant,
One is our God in the heavens and
the earth.

Shlosha mi yode'a,
Shlosha ani yode'a.
Shlosha avot,
shnei luchot habrit
echad elokeinu shebashamaim
uva'aretz.

Who knows three?
I know three:
Three are the fathers,
Two are the tablets of the covenant,
One is our God in the heavens and
the earth.

Arba mi yode'a
arba ani yode'a
arba imahot
Shlosha avot,
shnei luchot habrit
echad elokeinu shebashamaim
uva'aretz.

Who knows four?
I know four:
Four are the mothers,
Three are the fathers,
Two are the tablets of the covenant,
One is our God in the heavens and
the earth.

Chamisha, mi yode'a
Chamisha, ani yode'a
Chamisha chumshei torah
arba imahot
Shlosha avot,

Who knows five?
I know five:
Five are the books of the Torah,
Four are the mothers,
Three are the fathers,

shnei luchot habrit	Two are the tablets of the covenant,
echad elokeinu shebashamaim	One is our God in the heavens and
uva'aretz.	the earth.

Shisha, mi yode'a?	Who knows six?
Shisha, ani yode'a	I know six:
Shisha, sidre mishna	Six are the orders of the Mishnah,
Chamisha chumshei torah	Five are the books of the Torah,
arba imahot	Four are the mothers,
Shlosha avot,	Three are the fathers,
shnei luchot habrit	Two are the tablets of the covenant,
echad elokeinu shebashamaim	One is our God in the heavens and
uva'aretz.	the earth.

Shiv'ah mi yode'a	Who knows seven?
shiv'ah ani yode'a.	I know seven:
shiv'ah yemei shabatah	Seven are the days of the week,
Shisha, sidre mishna	Six are the orders of the Mishnah,
Chamisha chumshei torah	Five are the books of the Torah,
arba imahot	Four are the mothers,
Shlosha avot,	Three are the fathers,
shnei luchot habrit	Two are the tablets of the covenant,
echad elokeinu shebashamaim	One is our God in the heavens and
uva'aretz.	the earth.

Shmonah mi yode'a	Who knows eight?
shmonah ani yode'a	I know eight:
shmonah yemei milah	Eight are the days of circumcision,
shiv'ah yemei shabatah	Seven are the days of the week,
Shisha, sidre mishna	Six are the orders of the Mishnah,
Chamisha chumshei torah	Five are the books of the Torah,
arba imahot	Four are the mothers,
Shlosha avot,	Three are the fathers,
shnei luchot habrit	Two are the tablets of the covenant,

echad elokeinu shebashamaim uva'aretz.	One is our God in the heavens and the earth.
Tish'ah mi yode'a	Who knows nine?
tish'ah ani yode'a.	I know nine:
tish'ah chodshei leidah	Nine are the months of birth,
shmonah yemei milah	Eight are the days of circumcision,
shiv'ah yemei shabatah	Seven are the days of the week,
Shisha, sidre mishna	Six are the orders of the Mishnah,
Chamisha chumshei torah	Five are the books of the Torah,
arba imahot	Four are the mothers,
Shlosha avot,	Three are the fathers,
shnei luchot habrit	Two are the tablets of the covenant,
echad elokeinu shebashamaim uva'aretz.	One is our God in the heavens and the earth.
Asara mi yode'a	Who knows ten?
asara ani yode'a	I know ten:
asara dibraya	Ten are the statements,
tish'ah chodshei leidah	Nine are the months of birth,
shmonah yemei milah	Eight are the days of circumcision,
shiv'ah yemei shabatah	Seven are the days of the week,
Shisha, sidre mishna	Six are the orders of the Mishnah,
Chamisha chumshei torah	Five are the books of the Torah,
arba imahot	Four are the mothers,
Shlosha avot,	Three are the fathers,
shnei luchot habrit	Two are the tablets of the covenant,
echad elokeinu shebashamaim uva'aretz.	One is our God in the heavens and the earth.
Achad asar mi yode'a	Who knows eleven?
achad asar ani yode'a	I know eleven:
achad asar kochvaya	Eleven are the stars,
asara dibraya	Ten are the statements,

tish'ah chodshei leidah	Nine are the months of birth,
shmonah yemei milah	Eight are the days of circumcision,
shiv'ah yemei shabatah	Seven are the days of the week,
Shisha, sidre mishna	Six are the orders of the Mishnah,
Chamisha chumshei torah	Five are the books of the Torah,
arba imahot	Four are the mothers,
Shlosha avot,	Three are the fathers,
shnei luchot habrit	Two are the tablets of the covenant,
echad elokeinu shebashamaim	One is our God in the heavens and
uva'aretz.	the earth.

Shneim-asar mi yode'a	Who knows twelve?
shneim-asar ani yode'a	I know twelve:
shneim-asar shivtaya	Twelve are the tribes,
achad asar kochvaya	Eleven are the stars,
asara dibraya	Ten are the statements,
tish'ah chodshei leidah	Nine are the months of birth,
shmonah yemei milah	Eight are the days of circumcision,
shiv'ah yemei shabatah	Seven are the days of the week,
Shisha, sidre mishna	Six are the orders of the Mishnah,
Chamisha chumshei torah	Five are the books of the Torah,
arba imahot	Four are the mothers,
Shlosha avot,	Three are the fathers,
shnei luchot habrit	Two are the tablets of the covenant,
echad elokeinu shebashamaim	One is our God in the heavens and
uva'aretz.	the earth.

Shlosha-asar mi yode'a	Who knows thirteen?
Shlosha-asar ani yode'a	I know thirteen: thirteen are the
Shlosha-asar midaya	characteristics,
shneim-asar shivtaya	Twelve are the tribes,
achad asar kochvaya	Eleven are the stars,
asara dibraya	Ten are the statements,
tish'ah chodshei leidah	Nine are the months of birth,

shmonah yemei milah	Eight are the days of circumcision,
shiv'ah yemei shabatah	Seven are the days of the week,
Shisha, sidre mishna	Six are the orders of the Mishnah,
Chamisha chumshei torah	Five are the books of the Torah,
arba imahot	Four are the mothers,
Shlosha avot,	Three are the fathers,
shnei luchot habrit	Two are the tablets of the covenant,
echad elokeinu shebashamaim	One is our God in the heavens and
uva'aretz.	the earth.

SUPPLEMENTAL READING

Beitzah

THE ROASTED EGG OF PASSOVER
IS IT OF PAGAN ORIGIN?

*M*any people who have opted out of Christian holidays like Easter because of their dubious origins are uncomfortable with the idea of having a roasted egg as a symbol on the seder plate. They immediately associate it with the symbolism of pagan fertility rituals. However, once a person is familiar with the intimate details of the biblical sacrificial system that took place in the Holy Temple in Jerusalem, it becomes clear how this symbol is a perfect fit for the seder.

In the days of the Holy Temple, there were daily offerings that began and ended the daily functions of the priestly service. In addition to this, each of the special days of the year—Sabbaths and holy days—had additional offerings that were brought alongside the daily offerings. These are called the musaf, or "additional," offerings. Both of these offerings were communal offerings, meaning that they were not offered by individuals, but rather the community. There was another type of offering, however, that individuals could offer on certain holy days. This was called the chagigah, or "festive offering." There is an entire tractate in the Mishnah dedicated to clarifying the laws associated with it.

This offering is derived from a contradiction in the two passages in the Torah that describe the Pesach offering. Exodus 12 and Deuteronomy 16 give conflicting instructions regarding the offering to be given during this time:

> Tell all the congregation of Israel that on the tenth day of this month every man shall take a lamb according to their fathers' houses, a lamb for a household. And if the household is too small for a lamb, then he and his nearest neighbor shall take according to the number of persons; according to what each can eat you shall make your count for the lamb. Your lamb shall be without blemish, a male a year old. You may take it from the sheep or from the goats, and you shall keep it until the fourteenth day of this month, when the whole assembly of the congregation of Israel shall kill their lambs at twilight ... They shall eat the flesh that night, roasted (from צלה, tzalah) on the fire; with unleavened bread and bitter herbs they shall eat it. Do not eat any of it raw or boiled in water, but roasted (from צלה, tzalah), its head with its legs and its inner parts. (Exodus 12:3–6, 8–9)

> And you shall offer the Passover sacrifice to the LORD your God, from the flock or the herd, at the place that the LORD will choose, to make his name dwell there ... And you shall cook (from בשל, bashal) it and eat it at the place that the LORD your God will choose. (Deuteronomy 16:2, 7)

The problems between these two passages revolve mainly around two aspects of the Passover offerings. The first is that according to Exodus, the offering can only be "from the sheep or from the goats." However, the passage in Deuteronomy states that it may be "from the flock or the herd," implying that cattle are also an acceptable offering. The second problem is that Exodus restricts the method by which the offering may be cooked, saying that it may only be "roasted on fire," and not "boiled in water." The passage in Deuteronomy, however, uses the Hebrew word bashal, which has the primary meaning of boiling. Therefore, this second passage seems to permit boiling the meat, whereas the first one strictly prohibits it.

To resolve this we use the last of Rabbi Ishmael's Thirteen Principles of Interpretation, which says, "When two Biblical passages contradict each other the contradiction in question must be solved by reference to a third passage." Therefore, we find an example of how this conflict was resolved in the days of King Josiah:

> Josiah kept a Passover to the LORD in Jerusalem. And they slaughtered the Passover lamb on the fourteenth day of the first month ... Then Josiah contributed to the lay people, as Passover offerings for all who were present, lambs and young goats from the flock to the number of 30,000, and 3,000 bulls; these were from the king's possessions. 8 And his officials contributed willingly to the people, to the priests, and to the Levites. Hilkiah, Zechariah, and Jehiel, the chief officers of the house of God, gave to the priests for the Passover offerings 2,600 Passover lambs and 300 bulls. 9 Conaniah also, and Shemaiah and Nethanel his brothers, and Hashabiah and Jeiel and Jozabad, the chiefs of the Levites, gave to the Levites for the Passover offerings 5,000 lambs and young goats and 500 bulls ... And they roasted the Passover lamb with fire according to the rule; and they boiled the holy offerings in pots, in cauldrons, and in pans (2 Chronicles 35:1, 7–9, 13)

King Josiah and the people of his day understood these passage to refer to two separate offerings. It says, "They roasted the Passover lamb with fire according to the rule; and they boiled the holy offerings in pots, in cauldrons, and in pans" (2 Chronicles 35:13). Evidently, the actual Pesach offering was roasted, and the chagigah (in this case, bulls) was boiled. Therefore, the Talmud says that one should remember these two offerings at the seder:

> R. Joseph says, "There have to be two kinds of meat, one in memory of the Passover-offering, the other in memory of the chagigah (festive-offering)." (b.Pesachim 114b)

Since we are not to bring the actual offerings since the destruction of the Holy Temple,[2] there needed to be some way to ensure that the symbolic foods were not to be confused with the korban Pesach (Passover sacrifice) that can no longer be brought. Therefore, a roasted shank bone with some meat on it was used to represent the korban Pesach (and in some more recent traditions, a chicken neck is used to further distance the similarities between the two). But the chagigah posed a problem. How could we represent boiled meat without it seeming like we had actually participated in the actual event of boiling sacrificial meat? And also, how would one distinguish between the roasted meat and the boiled meat? It would be easier to represent the boiled meat with something that was commonly boiled and somewhat associated with meat such as an egg (although eggs are not considered meat according to halachah). An egg served perfectly for this purpose, because eggs are also a symbol of mourning. Why do we need a symbol of mourning on the seder plate? Because we are no longer able to enjoy the meat of the actual Passover offering, nor the sacrificial meat of its chagigah. We long for the day that the Holy Temple will be restored and we will be able to eat of the central components of the Passover with joy. The boiled egg on our seder plate is a constant reminder of the sacrificial meats we are no longer able to partake of.

How is the egg roasted and how did this roasting come in to play? The egg is usually boiled and then roasted in an open flame or placed in an oven until it begins to brown and crack. The roasting of the egg probably came about as a means to ensure that the egg was easily recognized for its symbolic representation, rather than simply being an additional food item at the meal. Another possibility why the egg is both boiled and roasted is that the chagigah could be offered by roasting or boiling, and so the two methods are combined and visibly noticeable in this symbol. ⚡

---

2   Deuteronomy 16:5–7

Ritual Hand Washing
SHOULD DISCIPLES OF YESHUA PARTICIPATE?

*M*any disciples of Yeshua tend to be uncomfortable with ritual hand washing. The first reason is because it may be an unfamiliar ritual and it simply feels awkward. This is perfectly fine and no one should be coerced into participation if they are uncomfortable. The second reason people may be uncomfortable when it comes to ritual hand washing may be for theological reasons. We hope that this brief article helps to alleviate this tension by shedding light on possible misunderstandings of key passages in the Apostolic Scriptures that seem to indicate Yeshua did not look favorably on ritual hand washing. However, if these arguments are still unsatisfactory, one should not feel pressured into participating in a ritual if they are troubled by it.

First let's talk about the core issue and the passages that have caused consternation over this matter. The primary concern by those who have theological objections to ritual hand washing, or Jewish ritual in general, is the belief that Jewish rituals and traditions are subverting the authority of the Scriptures. This is a legitimate concern that should not be taken lightly. Let's take a look at what Yeshua had to say about this matter.

The key passages that involve this issue are Matthew 15:1-20 and Mark 7:1-23. In both of the passages Yeshua and his disciples are criticized by a group of Pharisees because some of his disciples were "breaking the tradition of the elders" and eating with "unwashed hands." These passages are essentially identical, so we will focus on the details of Mark's account.

In Mark's account, it appeared to certain Pharisees "that some of his disciples ate with hands that were defiled, that is, unwashed" (Mark 7:2). One thing to note is that only some of Yeshua's disciples had foregone this ritual, implying others (including Yeshua) most likely did partake in its observance. So, they questioned Yeshua about this, saying, "Why do your disciples not walk according to the tradition of the elders, but eat with defiled hands?" (Mark 7:5). Yeshua replied by quoting a passage from Isaiah:

> Well did Isaiah prophesy of you hypocrites, as it is written, "This people honors me with their lips, but their heart is far from me; in vain do they worship me, teaching as doctrines the commandments of men" [Isaiah 29:13]. You leave the commandment of God and hold to the tradition of men. (Mark 7:6–8)

Yeshua continued his rebuke by saying:

> You have a fine way of rejecting the commandment of God in order to establish your tradition! For Moses said, "Honor your father and your mother"; and, "Whoever reviles father or mother must surely die." But you say, "If a man tells his father or his mother, 'Whatever you would have gained from me is Corban'" (that is, given to God)—then you no longer permit him to do anything for his father or mother, thus making void the word of God by your tradition that you have handed down. And many such things you do. (Mark 7:9–13)

Before we get into our explanation, let's work to understand a little about the origins of this tradition. Where did the ritual of hand washing originate and what is its significance? Both Matthew (15:1) and Mark (7:1) give us details about this particular group of Pharisees. It says that they "had come from Jerusalem." This is an important detail that is often left out of the discussion, but has an important bearing upon our understanding. Why is this important? Because it lets us know that these Pharisees were closely associated with the daily practices of ritual cleanliness that had developed within the observant Jewish community in and around Jerusalem during Yeshua's day. Because many of them were "daily in the Temple," similar to the disciples of the Master after his resurrection, ritual purity took on a higher status than among Jews living outside of the immediate vicinity of Jerusalem. Frequent visitation of the Temple would necessitate an almost constant state of ritual purity.

The practice of ritual hand washing developed within this context, based on the daily ritual of the priesthood as they ministered before the LORD. The reasoning behind the creation of this practice was a desire for the entire nation should all minister before Him in some capacity. This was not a novel idea of their own invention, but something expressed by God Himself. When Moses climbed Mount Sinai after leading the Israelites out of Egypt, the LORD revealed to him His desired purpose for the Children of Israel:

> If you will indeed obey my voice and keep my covenant, you shall be my treasured possession among all peoples, for all the earth is mine; and you shall be to me a kingdom of priests and a holy nation. These are the words that you shall speak to the people of Israel. (Exodus 19:5–6).

With this in mind, it was natural for those who were already working to maintain ritual purity to extend their practice to include additional rituals that mimicked those of the priesthood. The LORD had given the priesthood explicit instructions about the importance of ritually washing before entering into His service:

> When they go into the tent of meeting, or when they come near the altar to minister, to burn a food offering to the LORD, they shall wash with water, so that they may not die. They shall wash their hands and their feet, so that they may not die. It shall be a statute forever to them, even to him and to his offspring throughout their generations. (Exodus 30:20–21)

However, as important as ritual purity was for the priesthood, during the days of Yeshua it had become elevated to an unhealthy level. The Talmud records an account when two priests were competing over the performance of one of the duties in the Temple. As they were racing to their duties one took out a knife and stabbed the other in his jealousy. If this wasn't bad enough, what follows is unbelievable:

The father of the young man came and found him still in convulsions. He said: "May he be an atonement for you. My son is still in convulsions and the knife has not become unclean." [His remark] comes to teach you that the cleanness of their vessels was of greater concern to them even than the shedding of blood. Thus is it also said: Moreover Manasseh shed innocent blood very much, till he had filled Jerusalem from one end to the other. (b.Yoma 23a)

As we can see in this example, around the time of Yeshua ritual purity had taken precedent even over human life. Rabbi Simeon ben Eleazar noted this through a comment recorded for us in the Talmud saying, "Come and see how far purity has erupted in Israel!" (b.Shabbat 13a). Like Yeshua, Rabbi Simeon was commenting on the extremeness that some religious Jews were taking in relationship to ritual purity at the expense of more important commandments, even those regarding the sanctity of life.

Today, washing one's hands before eating bread is a common practice to commemorate both the ritual of the priestly duties within the Holy Temple, as well as the aspiration of becoming a nation of priests. Modern practice accentuates the sacrificial commemoration by sprinkling the bread with salt and a small score across the top of the loaf with a knife.

Many people feel that Yeshua's statements are a blanket statement about Jewish practice, and that following tradition, especially Jewish tradition, means going against Yeshua and his teachings. However, if we take a closer look at this example, we can see that Yeshua's issue was not against the ritual itself, but the hypocrisy of those pointing the finger at his disciples. Yeshua's rebuke was aimed at the elevation of a tradition above a commandment. In this particular case, it isn't that the tradition of ritual hand washing is bad, but that his opponents had more concern for the tradition than the observance of biblical instruction, such as honoring one's parents. They were quick to criticize the infraction of a tradition from others, but did not think twice about violating Scripture themselves.

A major question we need to ask is, "Does the practice of ritual hand washing violate or mistreat the Torah?" Yeshua chastised his opponents who elevated this ritual to the exclusion of the weightier matters of the Torah. However, since hand washing is based on symbolic application of a priestly function, in and of itself it does not violate Torah. Performing the ritual does not elevate tradition above Torah since it isn't replacing or negating any commandments, but can actually enhance and elevate the sensory experience of a religious expression.

Being educated in this matter may help one to overcome aversions that may have been based on incomplete information. If it will enhance your experience and draw you closer to the God of Israel, then there should be no reservation about its practice. If, however, one is still uncomfortable about participating, then one should not feel pressured into doing something against one's conscience. Ultimately, the decision to participate in ritual hand washing or not should be left up to the individual without any coercion in one direction or another. ✎

Karpas & Vinegar

Karpas is usually a green vegetable, commonly parsley, to remind us that Pesach occurs during the springtime of the year when the earth is fresh with new life. In many Passover seders it is tradition to dip the karpas into salt water. The salt water reminds us of both the tears which we shed while we were slaves and the Sea of Reeds through which we passed. Yet the salt water teaches us another important lesson. A life without the Messiah is truly a life immersed in tears. The karpas dipped into the salt water reminds us of what our lives were like when we were slaves.

However, a more ancient tradition is to use red wine vinegar in place of the salt water. Dipping the karpas into the red wine vinegar has many symbolic applications. The first correlation is to remember how the hyssop was dipped into the blood of the lamb and smeared onto the doorpost of the houses of the Israelite slaves. The second meaning is to remember how Joseph's coat was dipped into the blood of a goat. The jealousy of Joseph's coat lead his brothers to initiate their own family's descent into Egypt.

There is a third correlation, however, that takes us back to our Master's crucifixion. The combination of parsley (symbolic of hyssop) and red wine vinegar remind us of how he was given wine vinegar on a hyssop branch to quench his thirst:

> A jar full of sour wine stood there, so they put a sponge full of the sour wine on a hyssop branch and held it to his mouth. (John 19:29)

Our custom is to use parsley and red wine vinegar to remember these important aspects of our redemption. ⁂

Cup of Redemption Haggadah

OTHER GREAT RESOURCES
AVAILABLE FROM EMET HATORAH
Available on Amazon.com

The Four Responsibilities of a Disciple

Eight Lights: A Hanukkah Devotional for Followers of Yeshua

5 Minute Torah: Messianic Insights Into The Weekly Torah Portion

5 Minute Torah, Volume 2: Messianic Insights Into The Weekly Torah Portion
(August 2018)

Tefillot Tamid: Eternal Prayers from Jewish Tradition

Made in the USA
Middletown, DE
04 April 2018